30 Miracles in 30 Days

5 Easy Steps to Co-Creating
Unlimited Abundance,
Healing and Health
in All Areas of Your Life

by
Irene Lucas

PO Box 754, Huntsville, AR 72740
479-738-2348 www.ozarkmt.com

© 2009 by Irene Lucas

All rights reserved. No part of this book, in part or in whole, may be reproduced, transmitted or utilized in any form or by any means, electronic, photographic or mechanical, including photocopying, recording, or by any information storage and retrieval system without permission in writing from Ozark Mountain Publishing, Inc. except for brief quotations embodied in literary articles and reviews.

For permission, serialization, condensation, adaptions, or for our catalog of other publications, write to Ozark Mountain Publishing, Inc., P.O. Box 754, Huntsville, AR 72740, ATTN: Permissions Department.

Library of Congress Cataloging-in-Publication Data
Lucas, Irene, 1947-
   Thirty Miracles in Thirty Days, by Irene Lucas
Five simple steps to connect to the Divine and the Universe and co-create miracles.

1. Manifesting   2. Co-Creation   3. Meditation
I. Lucas, Irene, 1947-   II. Manifestation   III. Meditation   IV. Metaphysics
V. Title

Library of Congress Catalog Card Number: 2009934151

ISBN: 978-1-886940-65-9

Cover Art and Layout: www.enki3d.com
Book set in:Times New Roman, Lucida Calligraphy, Maiandra GD, Papyrus
Book Design: Julia Degan

Published by:

PO Box 754
Huntsville, AR 72740

WWW.OZARKMT.COM
Printed in the United States of America

A Universe of Endlessly Abundant Miracles

A child, looking thoughtfully into his half filled glass, was noticed by a man passing by.

"Well, little boy," said the amused passer by, "Is that glass half empty or half full?"

The child thought only a moment before he responded. "It doesn't matter if it's half empty or half full." The little boy beamed. "I can always go back for refills."

Tsen Tsing/I Lucas

Acknowledgments and Deepest Gratitude

★ My bright and radiant stars, my greatest, most spectacular blessings –you have each enriched my life beyond wildest imagination—the love of my life, my husband Louis, my glowing children, Dimitri and Alexander—you taught me what it really is to listen, love and be loved.

★ My heavenly, Divine Best Friends, my Celestial Army and Personal Cheering Squad--my ever faithful, ever patient, always with me, always fun and *humor-full* Buddies. For constant Divine inspiration, unwavering unconditional love and companionship, for never leaving me alone, and for sharing and inspiring limitless comfort, strength, courage, fun and laughter.

★ My dear friends and mentors Dawn and Darryl Schoenstadt – who first revealed the path to direct Divine connection to me and many more, and confirmed the *nearness* and not the far-ness of Spirit. You both offered your open hearts and taught us all how easy, swift and clear is the journey to connect to the Divine and to our Divine Buddies on our own.

★ CJ Scarlet—Gifted, inspired editor and writer in her own right -- my dear, devoted friend, inspired editor and supporter of this book and all my heart's desires.

★ My endlessly creative friends and co-workers Russell Shannon and Jackson Wheeler— I have been privileged to collaborate with each of you—your generosity of spirit and energy taught me how we can all use our gifts to open doors and offer love and support for others, known and unknown to us, and how the energy and passion of two equals the energy and passion of more than a million!

★ My Mom and Dad, James and Helen – for your daring and courage to leave a good life and journey to America and begin a new adventure, creating big open doors for all of us. Your unconditional love and compassion taught me how to stand up and stay strong. To my sister Penny -- we are still inseparable -- you will always be my buddy and best friend. All of you and your love remain brilliant and ever alive in my heart.

Table of Contents

Endlessly Abundant Miracles

Letter from our Friend Jesus   i

Author's Preface   ii

A Few Tips from Our Heavenly Friends   iv

Creating Sacred Spaces   vi

The Holy Breath   viii

Divine White Light
Totality (All the Colors)
of the Rays *to Clear the Path*   ix

Who Our Heavenly Friends Are and
What They Would like Us to Know about Them   xi

1	Peach Ray *Lady Quan Yin* *Divine Goddess* *of Mercy, Compassion* *and Charity*	*Divine Intervention*	1
2	Violet Flame *St. Germaine*	*Transmutation*	9
3	Pink Ray *Mother Mary* *Queen of Angels*	*Unconditional Love,* *Wisdom and Comfort*	15
4	Brilliant Pink Ray *Lady Quan Yin* *Divine Goddess* *of Mercy, Compassion* *and Charity*	*Forgiveness* *and Absolution*	21
5	Mauve Ray *Archangel Uriel* *Archangel of* *Transformation*	*Clarity of Intention*	27

6	Yellow Ray Archangel Jo(y)phiel Archangel of Illumination	Reactivation of Joy	33
7	Turquoise Ray Archangel Zoriah Archangel of the Brilliant Rainbow	Find an Oasis of Tranquility in the Midst of Inner and Outer Turmoil	39
8	Indigo Ray Archangel Uriel Archangel of Transformation	Success Reactivation; Release of Self Defeating, Self Destructive Behaviors and Obstacles; Knowledge of Self-Worth and Indwelling Faith; Re-connection to the ONE; Activation of Faith and Belief in Oneself; Heartiness and Resilience	47
9	Emerald Green Ray Archangel Raphael Archangel of Planetary and Personal Healing	Purity and Infilling of Abundance; Healing of Perception of Lack	53
10	Jade Green Ray Archangel Raphael Archangel of Planetary and Personal Healing	Internal and External Injuries	59
11	Golden Ray and the Christed Light Cosmic Buddha and Holy Master, Devoted Friend Jesus	Enlightenment, Compassion, Illumination, Unconditional Love; Joyfulness and Gratitude in Every Breath	65
12	Silver Ray Anarashia, Silver One As Jesus is to the Gold, Anarashia is to the Silver	Healing, Purity, Abundance and Joy	71
13	Orange Ray Archangel Jophiel Archangel of Illumination	Creativity	77

14	Auburn Ray Archangel Zoriel Messenger of God	*Instill and Awaken Organizational Skills and Abilities; Clearing, Cleansing, and Reorganization of Inner and Outer Clutter*	83
15	Aquamarine Ray Lady Quan Yin Divine Goddess of Mercy, Compassion and Charity	*Gentility and Grace, to Smooth and Make More Gentle the Healing Rays (Often used in partnership with other healing rays)*	91
16	Royal Deep Blue Ray Archangel Michael Archangel of Truth and Healing	*Peace and Prosperity*	95
17	Chartreuse Ray Archangel Michael Archangel of Truth and Healing	*Deeper into Discernment; Healing of Neglect*	99
18	Blue Ray Archangel Michael Archangel of Truth and Healing	*Truth, Justice, Clarity, Healing and Hope (Divine Confidence)*	105
19	Sky Blue Ray Archangel Michael Archangel of Truth and Healing	*Truth and Hope; Faith, Courage, Clarity*	111
20	Magenta Ray Archangel Uriel Archangel of Transformation	*Purity and Hope*	117
21	Crème Soft White/ Soft Yellow Rose Ray Mother Mary Queen of Angels	*Comfort, Empathy, Consideration, Thoughtfulness*	123

22	Lavender Ray *Lady Quan Yin* *Divine Goddess* *of Mercy, Compassion* *and Charity*	*Compassion and Nurturing*	131
23	Amber Ray *Lady Quan Yin* *Divine Goddess* *of Mercy, Compassion* *and Charity*	*Devotion;* *Healing of Disconnect and* *Indifference;* *Re-establishment of Awareness,* *of Connection in Prayer,* *and Connection and* *Communication* *with Spirit in Every Moment*	137
24	Navy Blue Ray *Archangel Uriel* *Archangel of* *Transformation*	*Healing and* *Elevation of Spirit*	143
25	Aqua Ray *Archangel Uriel* *Archangel of* *Transformation*	*Exaltation and Glory <u>in</u> Spirit* *Exaltation and Glory <u>of</u> Spirit* *We Are One with Spirit*	149
26	Red Ray *Archangel Uriel* *Archangel of* *Transformation*	*Courage, Faith, Truth, and* *Hope (Divine Confidence)*	155
27	Light Green Ray *Archangel Uriel* *Archangel of* *Transformation*	*Peace and Protection;* *Resolution of Conflict;* *Diminishing and Transmutation* *of Anger*	161
28	Dark Pink Ray *Archangel Zoriel* *Messenger of God*	*Healing of Depression*	169
29	Flame Orange Ray *Archangel Jophiel* *Archangel of* *Illumination*	*Healing of Indignity,* *Shame, and Burning* *Humiliation*	175

30	Platinum Ray *Holy Master,* *Devoted Friend Jesus* *Master Illuminator*	*Cleanse, Renew,* *Regenerate*	181
	Index	*Holy Masters,* *Archangels and* *Healing Rays*	187

A Letter from Our Friend Jesus

Beloveds, this is your _friend_ Jesus, not your Master Jesus. As we are all children of God, of Spirit, of the Universe, we are all connected.

Let us connect now, in love, in strength, in peace and in harmony for each of our individual healings, and our collective healing as ONE humanity and ONE race of people: all God's children.

My message to you about using these healing rays: **_simply accept the gift_**. Forget about whether you have "been good," or "are getting it". Especially forget your worry about whether you are worthy or not, or if this is the right time. I tell you now, because you hold this book in hand or hear this message, this is the most perfect time for you.

Forget about " getting it right or not getting it right". _You are getting it perfectly._

We in Spirit are all honored by your trust, your devotion, your faith, and we return it all a thousand fold, and many more times than that, back to you.

Allow us, then, to offer you this gift with our thanks, and our Divine love. As you pray to us for healings, _we in turn pray that you accept these Divine gifts, and accept yourselves as a Divine gift._

With our blessings, our Divine, unconditional love, our light, our knowledge and our promise that every moment in which you are holding these healings, you are in fact being healed –

Jesus and Your Heavenly Friends.

Author's Preface

Believe me, if I can do this, anybody can. If you can breathe, you can connect to the Divine.

You are always, already worthy. You are always, already holy. Whether you are aware of it or not, trust and faith are alive within you, awaiting your conscious reconnection to your Divine Friends.

We are all part of the ONE, each of us radiant with the spark of Spirit within. These pages and messages from Spirit and the Holy Masters serve to reveal and cultivate your own (already present!) gifts, offering tools to fan your Divine spark into the golden flames of your own radiant, miraculous Divine fire.

You do not need other people to connect to Spirit for you. Let go of the erroneous belief that "other people" are more worthy (gifted, have an inside track, special knack, etc.) than you. Even if you hold that belief, press on anyway. You will be thrilled when you discover what a beloved, worthy, Divine Co-creator and communicator with Spirit you (already) are.

I speak from experience. It seemed to me that someone else had a better connection, inside track, stronger gift. The journey in writing about Divine healing rays was almost entirely one of discovering my own truth, and my own gifts, and developing confidence in my own connection to the Divine. We each are always "getting it right"!

In these pages, **simple tools equal easy access.** Simple steps from the Holy Masters will help you to daily use affirmations, prayers and healing rays (you choose) to make great changes in your life. Give yourself the moments, a few in the morning and evening, which you need.

The healing rays are here to help your whole human self. In order to bring about shifts of energy, our Divine Friends, *with your permission,* guide their healing rays very deeply into the physical form, reawakening your very DNA.

You *are the creator,* **you** *are the initiator—the Holy Masters and Archangels, so eager and delighted to lovingly serve, are, even now, waiting for your invitation and permission.* Create your own Sacred Space (page vi), begin the Holy Breath (page viii), choose your healing ray(s) for the day, *and get going!*

A Few Tips from Our Heavenly Friends

The Holy Masters Offer These Suggestions:

- **Remind yourself I AM (already) ready and worthy.** No need, here, to perform a superhuman task to achieve worthiness, or to demonstrate faith. Even at this moment, whatever faith you have (even if you think you have none or almost none) is all the faith you need.

- **Breathe the Holy Breath.**

- **Choose your healing rays as you** desire—by the daily calendar sequence, the color of the ray, the Holy Master or Archangel, your intuition or need for a particular day. Presented as launching points, the prayers and affirmations accompanying each ray may be used with or without the healing rays (your choice).

- **Enjoy and absorb the healing ray with each breath.** Set your intention: pull the color and light of the healing ray into your heart center and lungs with each breath, during and following the meditation.

- **Envision the healing ray you have chosen** resting and radiating in your heart center, and with your every breath, emanating and blessing your entire being. An abundance of healing without limit is created! Declare your intention to allow, throughout the day, the healing light to flow and penetrate into all four bodies: physical, mental, emotional and spiritual, with each breath.

- **Hold the visual image** of the healing ray with which you are working. Perhaps you might use the image offered, or envision your own—keep the image in your awareness.

➢ ***Know yourself to be a walking rainbow of several healing rays working together at one time, in different ways. You can have it all.*** *You radiate a vibrational field of energy all around yourself—your aura.*

Divine energies from several different healing rays may radiate, actively healing, harmoniously in your aura. In addition, the healing ray within your heart center, which you have specifically chosen and with which you are consciously (physically, as well as in the emotional, mental and spiritual bodies) working is in your aura as well. Think of this rainbow of Divine Light(s) as a heavenly bonus!

➢ ***Perhaps you might wear something the same color as the Holy Ray you are working with each day***, to help you hold the vision and awareness of your Divine Friends and the Holy Light working so closely with you.

➢ ***Drink lots of water.***

As you read these pages, the Holy Masters ask you to remember basic truths about yourself: *HOLY I AM. WORTHY I AM. DIVINE INTERVENTION, I AM.*

You are the crucial co-participant in the miracles you are about to co-create with Spirit. Create, enjoy, notice, and be grateful and glad.

You have, in your hands, your own spiritual cook book for miracles.

I allow God to provide the ingredients, my soul to do the cooking, my mental, emotional, physical and spiritual selves to experience joy and delight. I AM glad and grateful for the feast.

A Note About Creating Sacred Spaces
in which to
Enjoy Prayers, Affirmations and Healing Rays

If you can breathe, you can bless and create!

A sacred space is more a state of mind and state of grace than a physical place. With a brief prayer and a breath, wherever you are, whatever your circumstances, call upon Spirit to (re)create your sacred space.

At the same time, in order to fully experience the healing rays, it is immensely helpful to have your own defined space (place, retreat). The more you use your "home base," the more powerful it becomes.

Honor yourself and your healing by preparing this place of stillness, of relative quiet, privacy, and most importantly, a place where you will not be disturbed or distracted, just for a few minutes a day.

Simplicity is the key. If you do not have a room, choose a corner of a room, the side of a couch, or whatever is available to you. Place an article signifying your connection to Spirit nearby—anything will do, as long as it has spiritual meaning to you. If possible, light a candle in this space as you prepare to receive the healing rays.

Find and commit to the space. Be aware: the space becomes committed, in turn, to serving you, by holding sacred energies.

The sacred space needs to be blessed and cleared of all energies except for the holy energies which you will call forth. Bless and clear each time you use your sacred space.

How to bless the space? In one moment, simple as one, two, three (no mumbo jumbo here).

1) Light a candle. *Energies in this room, I thank you, I bless you.*
2) Breathe Spirit in. *I call forth the St. Germaine and the Violet Flame of Transmutation.*
3) Breathe out. *I send all energies into the Violet Flame for transmutation.* Bless, breathe, and release energies into the Violet Flame of St. Germaine.

Can such a sacred clearing and blessing be accomplished, with such simplicity, in a moment? *Yes. You have a Celestial Army in your corner.*

Now, sit comfortably in your blessed space. The Holy Masters are your gatekeepers. You are safely enveloped and surrounded in Their Holy Light. The present moment is the perfect moment. Begin!

The Holy Breath

Change your Breath, change your life!
If you can breathe, you can heal!

The Holy Breath is the Breath of Spirit, of God. Breathe in, and breathe in Spirit, breathe in God. As deeply as you can, breathe in through your nose; then breathe out through your mouth. Breathe in as deeply and *comfortably* as you can from your diaphragm, breathe out as strongly as you are comfortably *able*.

As you breathe in God, you are refreshed, renewed, revived, infused with the Divine energies. Breathe out other energies (thoughts, experiences, contacts, stress, emotions)—envision your exhaling breath on a track of Divine Light, energies immediately blessed, transformed, returned to the Universe as Divine love.

Focusing on the Holy Breath helps to focus and move deeper into the meditation, healing you as you and your Divine Friends partner together. With keenly focused attention and interest on meditation, people (actually!) often forget to breathe. Remember to breathe the Holy Breath without pausing!

When you choose a healing ray, consciously breathe in the Divine color of the healing ray as you are moving through the meditation. Set your intention: with each breath, I AM breathing in the (color of) the healing ray, breathing Spirit into my heart center, in these meditation moments *and* throughout the entire day, whatever I AM doing, wherever my attention is focused.

Many classes and courses are available to refine the Holy Breath technique. The most important aspect for you in this moment: remember that *you are breathing in God, connecting to the Divine.*

Divine White Light: Let's Clear the Path

Much easier than you think! You can do this. The Divine White Light meditation is short, and may be done preceding each healing ray meditation.

Just breathe and focus.

Beloved Friends, let us clear the path to receive the Divine healing energies and the Divine holy rays which are our gift to you. As we clear the path, we open the doors in the mental, emotional, spiritual and physical bodies to be more receptive to the healing rays.

Begin the Holy Breath. If you lose focus, no big deal. Just begin the Holy Breath again. Sometimes, counting your breaths helps to stay focused. Breathe the Holy Breath in private as well as in public, as needed by simply setting your intention: *Spirit in, all else out.*

Find your sacred space. Stand or sit quietly, both feet on the ground. *Divine White Light, I call you forth at this time. I AM ready and worthy to receive Divine healing.*

Continue the Holy breath. Let the Divine White Light envelop you, encircle you, head to toe, within and without. Know yourself to be in a tube of loving White Light.

The White Light permeates and prepares all four bodies to be receptive to the healing ray of your choice.

Continue to breathe and envision the White Light spinning around you.

Envision the tube of White Light, starting from the top, going into every particle, every DNA strand of your body. Your mental, emotional, spiritual, as well as physical bodies are blessed and prepared by the White Light.

You do not force, compel, or will. *You simply allow.* Continue the Holy Breath. *I release. I let go. I let God.* You are now ready to choose your healing ray. You are standing (or sitting) in a tube of White Light, within and without. Enjoy your personal, friendly tornado. Choose your healing Ray. *Move forward.*

*Exactly Who Our Heavenly Friends Are
What They Would Like You to Know
About Each of Them
and
The Relationship They Desire to Enjoy
with You*

Ascended Masters and Goddesses

Different schools of thought focus on the Ascended Masters, with most in agreement. Ascended Masters are thought to have lived a lifetime or many lifetimes on the Earth. Through many incarnations, Ascended Masters gained all the knowledge and wisdom necessary for spiritual enlightenment and complete reconnection with the Source/Spirit/God. Examples are Mother Mary, Jesus, Saint Germaine, and Tsen Tsing the Cosmic Buddha, among many.

Via the ascension process, the Ascended Master (re)unites with His or Her own *God Self*, or the spark of God within, also known as the *I AM Presence*. Having fully realized the God within, and having fully ascended to join God/Source/ Spirit in the Heavenly and Universal realms, the Ascended Master, as the embodiment of unconditional Divine Love, is devoted to guiding, healing, loving, nurturing and teaching all life on Earth.

Great White Brotherhood or Great White Council

(Named for the brilliant White Light surrounding the Council, and having nothing to do with white males.) The Ascended Masters, male and female, collectively form the Great White Council because of the brilliant White Light aura which surrounds their energies.

Archangels

If we think of God/Source/Spirit as the President of University Earth, the Archangels are His Department Chair People, governing, nurturing, protecting, healing and teaching. Each Archangel has a specific area to oversee. For example, Archangel Michael is the Archangel of Truth and Justice, and Archangel Raphael is the Archangel of Personal and Planetary Healing.

Considered to be high ranking angels, Archangels are charged with the overview, nurturing and protection of various parts of the world, nature, nations, governments, humanity and all life, physical as well as spiritual. Archangels appear in many religions, including Judaism, Islam and Christian.

What our Heavenly Friends mean when they refer to all four bodies:

We each have a physical body, a mental body, an emotional body and a spiritual body.

MOTHER MARY
QUEEN OF ANGELS, MOTHER OF JESUS
Translation: *Divine unconditional love, Divine nurturing, Divine compassion*

Mother Mary would like you to know: *I am forgiving, and I can help you forgive that which you might think of as unforgivable—of yourself and others. I am endlessly compassionate. Call me forth for your children, and teach your children to call me forth in a simple breath, certainly in times of need, and also in times of celebration.*

The relationship Mother Mary desires to enjoy with you: *Instant, tender, miraculous, joyful, compassionate, steady, delightful, funny. Let's dance together, for ourselves and our children!*

Nurturing, compassion, infinite patience, grace and unconditional love, combined with a fierce passion to nurture and protect the children of this world, and those who love and care for them, characterize Mother Mary, Queen of Angels, and Mother of Jesus. As the Queen of Angels, Mother Mary often partners as a (co)miracle worker in support of other angels and Archangels.

Mother Mary is a passionate protector of all children. She loves to perform miracles. She enables everyone who is connected to a child to be patient and to express and experience unconditional love, compassion, wisdom and an open, nurturing heart. Seen by children, Mother Mary is often surrounded by pink roses. We can sometimes know that she is near by the fragrance of roses. Mother Mary also loves to dance, and plays with children wherever they are.

Historical researchers disagree on Mary's early life. The Four Gospels of the Bible tell us that Mary grew up in a "working class" village of Nazareth, and married the carpenter Joseph. Biblical scholars represent the other four sons and one daughter were Joseph's from his first marriage. Divinely inspired information offers a different view—that the other five children in addition to Jesus were those of Mary and Joseph. Divinely inspired information also offers the view that Mary took Jesus to live with the Essenes where both Jesus and Mary learned many mystical and metaphysical secrets.

LADY QUAN YIN
DIVINE GODDESS OF MERCY, COMPASSION AND CHARITY

Translation: *She who hears the cries of the world, She who hears prayers, or She who is always listening.*

Lady Quan Yin would like you to know:
I love you unconditionally. I do not judge you. It doesn't matter to me where you have been or where you are going, what you do or have done, where you live or whether you have wealth. All that matters to me is that you know I love you. I have always loved you, in this and other lives, and I always will love you.

The relationship Lady Quan Yin desires to enjoy with you:
We are miracle makers together. I am here to serve you as your steadfast friend. Best buddies, just a breath and a call away. I offer you hope (Divine confidence), love and joy.

Lady Quan Yin is the embodiment of unconditional love, kindness, compassion and mercy. She is constantly listening to all of our prayers. One of the most popular and beloved Divine Energies and Goddesses in the tradition of Buddhism, Lady Quan Yin is considered the "Eastern" or Buddhist counterpart to the

"Western" Mother Mary. Both embody Goddess and Divine Mother energies of unconditional love, nurturing and compassion. She is also associated with the loving and helpful Tibetan Buddhist Goddess Tara. Lady Quan Yin is often represented as carrying pearls of illumination, the lotus flower of unconditional love, or pouring streams of healing water.

Buddhist monks have a wonderful description of Lady Quan Yin's limitless compassion and mission to end suffering in our world. Having attained enlightenment, Lady Quan Yin was preparing to cross the threshold into Nirvana, when she heard all the cries of the world. At that moment, Lady Quan Yin vowed to remain in service to humanity, until each and every soul is liberated, joyful, and reconnected to their God-Source.

ARCHANGEL URIEL
ARCHANGEL OF TRANSFORMATION
Translation: *Flame of God, God's Light, Light of God*

Archangel Uriel would like you to know:
I am (my transformations are) not to be feared! Embrace me and all that I offer to enrich your life. Together, let's transform poverty and limitation into limitless abundance, in all levels and in all four bodies.* Easier than you think! No harm comes from Divine transformation—only love and increase.

The relationship Archangel Uriel desires to enjoy with you:
Liberation. Call on me as your liberator. One breath, one moment, and I am with you, to lovingly serve you.

Moving us from confusion and darkness into bliss and light, Uriel is the Archangel of Transformation. He views His job description as *"Transforming every soul, every being, every situation and condition out of darkness, turmoil, out of limitation, into crystal clear light, wisdom and understanding of our connection to the ONE."* Uriel's mission is the transformation of the planet and humanity—one cell, one person, one soul, one raindrop at a time.

Faith, hope, vision, self-confidence and self-awareness are restored and resurrected by Archangel Uriel. Are you in search of a reconnection to the ONE? Are you feeling muddled and do you seek clarity of intention? Give a holler to Archangel Uriel—he is listening and waiting for your invitation. The next time you are down on yourself, invite Him to remind you who you really are.

*Archangel Uriel frequently refers to all four bodies, as do the other Archangels and Ascended Masters and Goddesses. The four bodies include our mental body, physical body, emotional body and spiritual body.

SAINT GERMAINE
Also known as the Count of Saint Germaine
Ascended Master (not a Saint)

Saint Germaine would like you to know: *I came here to have fun, by God, and I did it, and I would do it again, gladly. Meantime, let's have some fun together. Now, this minute, as you read this, think of something fun to do and do it! Let's get heart, soul, mind and body together to more fully reconnect. I throw a few reminders your way.*

The relationship Saint Germaine desires to share with you: *A Divine and constant partnership of imploding and exploding fun.*

Hilarious, bigger than life, compelling, jolting, tender, stern, forever loving unconditionally, Saint Germaine is a friendly, accessible, and an incredibly humorous Ascended Master. He often advises us to have ***FUN***. Saint Germaine is an integral part of the Great White Brotherhood (named because of the radiant, Divine White Light surrounding the members of the Council; certainly not connected to white males!).

During his lifetime(s) on Earth, the Count Saint Germaine demonstrated stunning talents and abilities, including the ability to communicate in many languages, musical virtuosity, artist (painter), and mystical powers of prophecy and alchemy. He was a powerful political force on behalf of justice, both in France and in the creation of the American Declaration of Independence. Divinely inspired beliefs place Him among us in the past as Shakespeare, Merlin, Christopher Columbus, and Thomas Jefferson, among others. Saint Germaine loves to be mysterious.

Saint Germaine offers the *Violet Flame of Transmutation*. Whenever you have a negative thought or experience, Saint Germaine encourages you to visualize a *Violet Flame* in front of you, breathe in Spirit, and breathe out the negativity into the *Violet Flame*. The *Violet Flame of Transmutation* transmutes and transforms the negativity into Universal love, returning positive, loving energy into the Universe.

"Pay attention. Be aware," counsels Saint Germaine. *"Be very aware."* Encouraging us to have fun, Saint Germaine asks us also to notice the joy in our lives, and pay attention to the way our government treats people—fairly or unfairly. He asks us to keep an active and vigilant approach towards justice and peace, advocating for those without a social, political, or economic voice. *"Keep the good guys in office,"* our humorous Friend suggests. *"Be busy where it counts."* He asks us to consider prosperity and abundance, *"and the pursuit of happiness, with liberty and justice for all."*

ARCHANGEL MICHAEL
ARCHANGEL OF TRUTH AND HEALING

Translation: *He who is like God, He who is as God, He who looks like God*

Archangel Michael would like you to know:
I cut away the illusions binding you in fear, and reveal to you your own courage and strength. I open the doors and clear the path for you to do your true work and know who you are. I am your personal, celestial army.

The relationship Archangel Michael desires to enjoy with you:
I am your champion, I am instantly with you. Let us be constant together. Let us be intrepid together.

Archangel Michael is our passionate, intense champion, truly our knight in shining armor, cutting away the ties and strings of attachment and illusion with his flaming Blue Sword of Truth. In addition to being our champion and protector, in all aspects of our lives, Archangel Michael can be considered to be our celestial "bodyguard". Call his name and He is instantly at your side, spiritual sword drawn, in any physical, emotional, mental, or even spiritual challenge.

Often represented as a warrior angel, Archangel Michael fights and triumphs on behalf of justice and truth. In fact, Archangel Michael's name is said to have been the war cry of heavenly angels in their battle against Satan and his followers.

Ever courageous, Archangel Michael is also considered to be the Patron Saint, along with Saint George, of chivalry, daring and courage, intervening to right wrongs, uncover the truth and effect justice. He is also the Patron Saint of police officers and soldiers. If a person is stuck, fearful, confused about their life's path,

Archangel Michael can step in, cut away the cumbersome and misleading illusions, and reveal the path of light and courage.

ARCHANGEL RAPHAEL
ARCHANGEL OF PLANETARY AND PERSONAL HEALING
Translation: *God has healed, God heals*

Archangel Raphael would like you to know:
From little cuts and bruises to the most terrible and traumatic injury or illness, I AM with you. I await your invitation in any moment to begin the healing process. Instantly. I love you.

The relationship Archangel Raphael desires to enjoy with you:
Constancy. Keep me in your back pocket, call me when you need me—I'll be there with great joy to serve you.

Archangel Raphael is the Divine Physician. If you have an internal or external injury or an illness, invite Archangel Raphael and his Emerald Green Ray of Healing. Charged with healing the injuries and illnesses of humanity and animals on planet Earth, Archangel Raphael also heals spirit and soul. *"It's a big job,"* Archangel Raphael offers with a smile, *"and I can do it. Just give me a cosmic ring. No waiting!"*

A cosmic ring, according to Archangel Raphael, is accomplished with a heartfelt invitation and a breath and a prayer, as short as, *"Archangel Raphael, I invite you in this moment."*

From Western to Eastern medicine, from the most remote, isolated valley to the foremost urban high-tech hospital,

Archangel Raphael works closely with healers in all cultures and forms. The patient has merely to invite Him to inspire and guide the physician or healer.

ARCHANGEL JOPHIEL
Also known as ARCHANGEL JOY-PHIEL
ARCHANGEL OF ILLUMINATION
Translation: *Beauty of God*

What Archangel Jophiel would like you to know:
I open the doors to wonder and wondrous creativity. You are simply amazed at what you already have within you, and I am privileged to reveal to you your gifts. No wonder I am joyous!

The relationship Archangel Jophiel desires to enjoy with you:
You are in constant discovery of the wondrous gifts of Spirit which you have, and I am constantly with you, offering you the key to unlock one treasure after another after another of limitless light and knowledge.

A joyful and passionate teacher, Archangel Jophiel is the great illuminator, helping us to discover our own gifts of creativity and joy, and inspiring us to seek and realize spiritual experiences, realities and miracles. Archangel Jophiel also asks us to seek and notice beauty within ourselves and others, and to open our eyes, ears and hearts to enjoy the beauty of the world on all levels, in all relationships—from bugs to beloveds.

If your heart's desire is to acquire more knowledge and wisdom, open to a deeper, clearer intuition, and enjoy more joy and laughter in your life, Archangel Jophiel is delighted to serve you.

Wherever learning is happening, Archangel Jophiel is nearby, clearing the path to wisdom and supporting knowledge of every kind. Perhaps you are stuck half way through a project. Happy when you started, but too discouraged or disinterested to finish? Perhaps you can't even get started! From plumbing to astronomy, with all artistic and other endeavors in between, call upon Archangel Jophiel for a joyous inspiration and energy to finish up successfully and move on.

Are you a student, disheartened and exhausted, studying for final exams, needing to truly absorb and comprehend the material you are studying? Invite Archangel Jophiel to study with you. If you've got the willies about the taking the final exam, invite Jophiel to pull up a chair right next to you. He will offer Divine energy to help you to be aware and express the knowledge which you already learned. Perhaps you may be feeling unsettled about a job interview or presentation—you get the picture. Archangel Jophiel, suited up, accompanies, encourages and sees you through with Divine energy, enabling you to shine your light brightly.

If you are feeling sad, Archangel Jophiel invites you to fall back into His wings for comfort and the resurrection of joy. If you are stuck, in any form, physical, mental, emotional or spiritual, stand up and lean on His wings and receive a loving embrace to reignite your joy.

ARCHANGEL ZORIAH
ARCHANGEL OF THE BRILLIANT RAINBOW
Translation: *Peace and Contentment*

Archangel Zoriah would like you to know:
Do not grasp and struggle in the air between two mountains, plummeting, terrified, down through space. Invite me into your heart, allow me to build you a solid bridge for your sure footing and refuge—the rest will follow. I use strands and planks of unconditional love, woven and built with strength and courage, wisdom and gratitude. Our bridge, our refuge, is radiantly colored beyond imagination, with each color offering its own healing power and gift to you. Find your firm and solid footing here, my children, and you will find your inner wisdom and courage. First of all, you will find your peace.

The relationship Archangel Zoriah desires to enjoy with you:
I AM with you all the time. I AM only a breath away. Healing, instantaneous and intense. Do not believe that you need to wait for darkness to fall on you, for your heart to break in two, or for your mind to feel splintered. At the first sign of anxiety, stress, dis-peace, call upon me and I am with you instantly! Make me your first 911 call. I arrive before you know it, and healing begins immediately. My arms are already open to enfold you, beloved.

I AM Archangel Zoriah, a messenger of God. I am a behind the scenes Archangel. I AM less known than my beloved compatriots in the heavenly realms. Whether or not you are familiar with me is unimportant. Beloveds, it is my mission which is important to you. My mission is to bring peace and contentment to ravaged hearts during moments of turmoil. In any moment, in any place, when you might experience slight to overwhelming turmoil, I offer you my Turquoise Light to soothe each cell, each part of you mind, body and soul.

ARCHANGEL ZORIEL
MESSENGER OF GOD
Translation: *Compelling and Distinct*

Archangel Zoriel would like you to know:
The time has come to clear out the old to make room for the new. In your home, your office, your property. Also in your physical body, mind, emotional body and soul. We can do this together, simply, freely, and have some fun at the same time! While you may not know me now, check me out and see what grand friends we become!

The relationship Archangel Zoriel desires to share with you:
Clarity, clarity, clarity, on every level. Clear vision, clear vision, clear vision, on every level. Inner and outer! Let's clear the path and begin a fresh start together.

I do not abandon you. I see you through to the glorious goals you set for yourself and your physical surroundings, with Divine inspiration.

Do you wonder who I might be? Am I obscure to you? I am Archangel Zoriel, Messenger of God. My mission is to deliver uplifting energies of Divine unconditional love and Divinely glorious clearing of your inner and outer space. We make room for the uplifting, joyous and creative energies multiplied many thousands of times over! Start your life over as many times as you need to—I am with you!

ANARASHIA THE SILVER ONE
AS JESUS IS TO THE GOLD, ANARASHIA IS TO THE SILVER
Translation: *Beauty, Grace, Sharp Intensity*

Anarashia would like you to know:
My beloveds, I am truly at your service. Like any great lady, I can not attend without your invitation.

The relationship Anarashia desires to share with you:
One of love, beloveds. Devotion, dedication and service to you, and I desire your awareness of me—invite me to the party of your life. Experience our healing, mutual devotion and commitment – a relationship of joy and radiance, in all four bodies (mental, emotional, physical and spiritual).

I AM the Goddess Anarashia. I AM part of God, part of the ONE, as you are. As Jesus radiates Divine, bright, Golden Light, I radiate Divine, bright, Silver Light. We both accompany Source, God, Spirit. Likely I am unknown to you. My gifts and my Sliver Light however, are well known to you—healing, abundance, joy and reconnection to Spirit (which you call purity).

It is my desire that you call me forward whenever you need a sharp, laser like healing—instantly, or over a period of time, as you desire. With laser point accuracy, I resurrect, resuscitate, regenerate, renew your cells and spirit which seek healing, renewal, abundance and joy.

JESUS and the CHRISTED LIGHT

Also referred to *as Jesus Christ, Lord and Savior, Jeshua, Yeshua,*
Lord Jesus, Sanada
Translation of Jesus: *Salvation*
Translation of Christed Light: *Light of the Anointed One*

Jesus would like you to know:
I AM not your Master Jesus, but your Friend Jesus. I love you. Always have and always will. Think of me as your best friend. Call upon me. Instantly, I am with you. I AM actually fun to be with. Let's get on equal footing, stay there, and dance a little together. All the time. Why wait?

The relationship Jesus desires to enjoy with you: *Constant and instant, with my love and healing penetrating your heart and soul, as you have penetrated my heart and soul. Let's get going!*
  We'll go together to wonderful places of peace, joy and abundance beyond imagination. Always remember who your Friends are.

Considered in Christian religions to be the Son of God, Jesus is the embodiment of healing in action, faith in action, compassion in action, miracles in action, forgiveness in action, good humor and wit in action, and limitless unconditional love in action. Jesus does not exclusively limit his love to the devoted members of the Christian religions. Baptists, Taoists, agnostics and atheists—every living being—are all equally loved and treasured by Jesus.

In *30 MIRACLES IN 30 DAYS*, Jesus and the Cosmic Buddha demonstrate their unlimited, unconditional love for one another and for humanity, without religious requirements or criteria, by forming a circle together and spiritually holding hands with one another and with you, the reader, offering their Divine energies.

His message at this moment is simply to love one another, be kind to one another, and remember who you are and your connection to Spirit. Jesus wants us to know that we each carry a spark of God/Spirit/Source within us, that we each are in fact part of the ONE. Whether a person has incredible, unbending faith, only the most microscopic shred of faith or sincere skepticism—Jesus responds to all who desire and ask, with an open heart, for guidance, companionship and miracles.

COSMIC BUDDHA AND TSEN TSING
(different names for the same Ascended Master)
Translation: *Enlightened One, or Awakened One*

The Cosmic Buddha/Tsen Tsing would like you to know:
*Be alert, very alert. Be aware, very aware—of your timing, your lives. Each breath you take is **a gift from God**. Each breath you take is also a **gift given to God**, if you so choose. Simply declare your intention. Have fun, shout with laughter, and in the proper moment—perhaps just a couple of moments each day, breathe deeply three times, remain quiet and listen, so that my messages to you, my beloveds, can be heard by you. Humanity, as we all know it, is at this moment in desperate need of your spirit, your vitality, your love and your good energies. Humanity is also in great need of your authenticity and ability to receive, offer, experience and express JOY! JOY! JOY!*

The relationship Cosmic Buddha/Tsen Tsing desires to enjoy with you:
A listening relationship. I am near. I offer loving thoughts, guidance, and answers to your questions. So long for this moment, beloveds. Let me hear from you—that you may hear from me!

I was created before time as you know it, as a breath and a spark of God, of Spirit, of Source –I always was, always will be. I am not specifically the Buddha which you know as our beloved Siddartha, though we are all equally a spark of God. I AM part of God, with God, as are you. Since I arrived before time, I have no historical context to which you can relate.

I am also known as Tsen Tsing—Holy, I AM your brother! Up in the mountains of Tibet, in the time you might know as 5000 or 6000 BC, we created a form Buddhism to express our love for humanity and for Spirit. We had quite a wonderful world up there. I now serve you from heavenly realms, which are even a more fun world. You can share our heavenly realms here on Earth, with a breath and an invitation to us.

Cosmic Buddha loves all beings unconditionally, from Shinto to Christian, agonistic and atheist alike. In the last chapter of *30 MIRACLES IN 30 DAYS*, He joins hands with His beloved friend Jesus and you, the reader, to form a circle of Golden Light to uplift and recharge you with the vitality of unconditional, radiant love.

Chapter One

Peach Ray: Invite and Experience Divine Intervention
Lady Quan Yin, Divine Goddess of Mercy, Compassion and Charity

Divine intervention: don't leave home without it. The more, the merrier.

Opening Affirmation

I AM worthy to receive Divine Intervention. I AM Divine Intervention. I trust the power of Divine Intervention to get the job done. I discern and I AM thankful for each miracle.

Opening Prayer

I invite You, Lady Quan Yin, and the Peach Ray to help me invite and access the experience Divine Intervention, Divine compassion, Divine creativity and Divine power. Through my own holiest and Divine energies, focus my eyes with clarity, to see that which needs to be seen. Sharpen my hearing that I may listen to that which I need to hear, to discern the needs, hopes and desires of my own self and those of whom I AM aware. I call upon the holiest of energies within and without. Lady Quan Yin, Peach Ray of Divine Intervention, I invite you in this moment to co-create miracles with my Divine self. I seek discernment and clarity of intention to more clearly initiate and manifest miracles. Make keen my awareness to discern, with every breath, the miracles around me, and to know that I AM a miracle in action. I seek not only to serve myself, but others as well.

Invitation and Permission

I invite Lady Quan Yin and the Peach Ray to invite and experience Divine Intervention into my heart, my soul, and all four bodies. I give my permission to fully allow Lady Quan Yin to direct the Peach Ray to any part of all four bodies: physical, mental, spiritual and emotional, where it is most needed. I allow the Divine Peach Ray to reawaken the DNA in my physical body.

Spirit does not depend upon. Spirit IS. The presence of Spirit is constant and consistent, not dependent upon your conscious awareness of Spirit. *The unconditional love of Spirit is always with you, whether you know it or not and whether you accept it or not.*

Even though we live our lives within the radiance of our own consciousness of Spirit, we often need to call forth and request Divine Intervention. At these times, the gentle yet powerful and laser-intense energies of Lady Quan Yin and Her Peach Ray (re)awaken our own internal Divinity and Divine abilities to co-create Divine Intervention.

The Peach Ray reawakens the miraculous I AM energies, alerting each cell and DNA strand not only to *accept* the energies of God/Goddess I AM, but to be aware that each cell and DNA strand *is* God/Goddess I AM.

The invitation to Divine Intervention is a three step process.

First, we (re)awaken and become aware of our own Divine self and abilities to co-create Divinely.

Second, we discern the clarity of our intention: define the situation, present to Spirit the intention.

Third, notice and accept the miracle and the healing.

Enjoy your Co-created miracle! Express the gratitude you feel!

Peach Ray: Invite and Experience Divine Intervention

Divine Intervention is a deeper expression of each of our own Divine selves. Divine Intervention is simply another expression for a miracle, **except this time you are *not only noticing the process, you are a co-creator of the process*.** How grand and how strong you are!

Lady Quan Yin offers you Her special gift of the Peach Ray, to smooth the path, offering a practical tool to Co-create Divine Intervention. *Focus your Divine awareness, Divine intention and Divine energies.* Indeed, you are the crucial participant.

We begin the meditation. Seek your sacred space. Begin the Holy Breath. Comfortable, deep breaths, in through the nose, out through the mouth. *You are co-creator with Spirit.*

Lady Quan Yin, I invite you, Divine Goddess of Mercy, Compassion and Charity, and your Peach Ray of Divine Intervention to be with me at this time. I request, I initiate, I AM part of the miracle. Holy I AM. Worthy I AM. Visualize the most luscious peach you have ever seen. The colors are soft orange and delicate, almost invisible yellow. Imagine the sweetness.

Breathe in and feel the light and power of Lady Quan Yin as she enfolds you with loving energies. *Lady Quan Yin, thank you for enfolding me with your energies and the Peach Ray of Divine Intervention.*

As you continue to breathe in the energies of the Peach Ray, continue to be aware of the loving, enfolding presence of Lady Quan Yin, and the soft, powerful orange yellow colors.

The Peach Ray is with you, radiating, radiating. Breathe in the Peach Ray as a fine mist.

The first step—we awaken your Divine self to co-create Divinely. *The light of the Peach Ray, radiating within you, is awakening, reminding, alerting each of your cells, to their very DNA fiber: I AM. I AM Divine.*

I AM Divine Intervention. The soft Orange Yellow Light continues, cell by cell, DNA strand by DNA strand, to revive and awaken your own Divinity.

Continue to breathe. The Peach Ray is reawakening, with gentle but powerful laser precision, each and every I AM DNA strand with knowledge of your holiness; knowledge of your Divinity; knowledge of your worthiness; knowledge of your Divine power and participation in each miracle, in each Divine Intervention.

Continue to breathe: *I AM. Holy I AM. Worthy co-creator I AM. Divine I AM. Holy, Divine power I AM. Divine ability I AM. Divine participant I AM.*

Continue to breathe. With every breath, feel the radiance as the Peach Ray continues to expand within you. The radiance and light of the Peach Ray continues to alert the I AM cells to their Divinity and Divine abilities.

Eyes to see with Divine clarity, intention and discernment. Continue to breathe and feel the soft Peach Light expand lovingly, yet powerfully. *Ears to hear and listen with Divine clarity, intention and discernment.*

Continue to breathe. *Mouth to speak the truth with Divine clarity, intention and discernment. Throat to form the voice of Divine clarity, intention and discernment.*

The radiant Peach Ray glows around and within you. Even your fingertips pulsate with the energy. Continue to breathe.

The luminous warmth shimmers in your heart area, resting, reminding your heart of your heart's Divinity.

With every breath, feel the radiance of the Peach Ray, moving slowly, guided by Lady Quan Yin, reminding each cell *I AM Divine.*

Continue to breathe as the Peach Ray expands to the solar plexus, all the way down to the root chakra. The Peach Ray will pause and rest where needed, and then continue.

Your first step is complete—your cells, even to your very DNA, have been reawakened with the knowledge of their own Divinity and Divine abilities: of being Co-Creators of the Divine.

I AM Holy. I AM Divine. I AM Divine power. I AM Divine Intervention.

Continue with the second step: *Clarity of Intention. We clearly define our intention and purpose.*
Continue the Holy Breath. Notice the strength of the Peach Ray and the energies of Lady Quan Yin holding and supporting you.

Raise the situation for which you seek Divine Intervention. Ask for clarity of intention and discernment. What do I really want? Define the situation, the desire.

Speak or write your situation, your desire. Spirit, I ask for Divine Intervention, mindful that I AM the co-creator of Divine Intervention. *I trust my own Divine being, at the deepest level, to co-create together with Spirit, the best of all possible outcomes.*

Continue to breathe. A reminder, beloved masters: it is *not your role to control* the resolution of your situation. Your role is to 1) discern your purpose; 2) clarify your intention; 3) initiate the miracle you are co-creating Divinely with clarity. Inform Spirit and the Universe of your intention, and participate Divinely.

Continue to breathe. The soft Orange Yellow Light of the Peach Ray continues to rest within you. Lady Quan Yin continues to lovingly support you.

The Peach Ray, seeking your deepest soul desires, continues to imbue each cell with Divine clarity of intention and purpose, revealing, co-creating your miracle.

Continue to breathe in the Peach Ray as a fine mist. Allow your Divine *I AM* to discern the truth of your situation, enabling you to more clearly present your intention to the Universe, to Spirit. *Define your purpose, your intention.*

Your intentions and purpose, even more than your situation, require clarity. What is the purpose? What is the outcome? It is the clarity of intention you seek when you ask for this miracle and which the Universe awaits. *Clarity of intention is in itself part of the miracle.*

(For example, I need Divine Intervention to sell my house—a description of a situation. Clarity of intention: to leave present surroundings, to release that which is holding me back, gaining fairly in the sale of the home, *to begin a new, Divinely inspired and abundant life in new surroundings).* Your intention and the energies of the situation are not separate.

I AM Divine Intention. Each time I move, each time I breathe, I act with Divine Intention. Lay the issue upon the feast table of Spirit. Allow Spirit, in turn, to present the feast to you.

Continue the Holy Breath. Beloved Spirit, this is the situation at hand, *these are my intentions.* I invite, I AM, the *Co-creator of Divine Intervention.* Continue to breathe.

Spirit, I trust and await the miracle we have Co-created. Lovingly, you are asking for the outcome, not directing, defining or controlling. Trust Spirit and your own Divine self to see the big picture and to surprise you with the most perfect miraculous result. The miracle and Divine Intervention are complete, ready to manifest.

The healing and miracle are already moving up the road to meet you, for you to enjoy, acknowledge and experience.

Worthy I AM. Holy I AM. Open I AM to receive and notice the glories, experiences and miracles of Divine Intervention. I AM the miracle. I AM Divine Intervention.

The third step in the process, beloveds, as important as the first two: notice the miracle, offer acceptance, recognition and thanks. Be on the lookout for the miracle(s) manifesting! Be aware—*be very aware!* Be alert to the unfolding of the miracle—the Divine Intervention—in each expected and unexpected expression of the miracle manifesting. Be thankful. Express gratitude.

Fully acknowledge inner and outer Spirit: your own reawakened (inner) Divinity and the Divine Spirit as Co-Creators of the miracles. Enjoy the fruits of the Divine Intervention, the feast of miracles presented to you.

The miracles are endless, abundant, as is the Divine love of Spirit. Get ready for the next miracle—Divine Intervention—do it again!

Closing Affirmation
Clarity of Intention I AM. Divine abilities, Divine miracles, I AM. Co-creator of Divine Intervention and miracles, I AM.

Closing Prayer
Thank you for reawakening, reviving my internal Divine abilities to Co-create miracles; to be a participant in Divine Intervention. Please help me to keep my thoughts, my eyes, my heart open to only the deepest, most Divine level of discernment and clarity; and the highest most excellent level of intention that I may continue to discern opportunities for Divine Intervention, and continue to manifest and co-create miracles on my behalf, and in the holiest love on behalf of others.

Author's note: I was privileged to feel Lady Quan Yin enfold me with her energies—a very powerful sense of her right behind me, enveloping me, holding and offering her energies.

I could feel Lady Quan Yin's Peach Ray enter from the right side, expanding as the process continued. The pulsating and tingling in my fingertips and the warmth were very reassuring.

I could feel a pretty good sense of where the Peach Ray was working. I was challenged at the point of determining the clarity of intention and purpose, versus simply stating the situation and asking for what seemed to be an obvious outcome.

I had to pause to consider, ask for Divine guidance, about the true clarity of my intention.

Chapter Two

Violet Flame of Transmutation
Saint Germaine and the Heavenly Parties

Synchronization with Spirit.
Let us be authentic. Let us synchronize with Spirit.

Image: The Violet Flame before you.

Opening Affirmation
I Am liberated as I place into the Violet Flame all energies which do not serve personally and globally, in all moments, for transmutation into the glorious and the Divine.

Opening Prayer
St. Germaine, I AM ready for more FUN in all aspects of my life, in all four bodies. I invite you and the Violet Flame of Transmutation to co-liberate me from negative energies which are holding me down. Uplift and free my soul, my mental, emotional and physical bodies to enjoy more joy, as I place all energies which do not serve into the Violet Flame of Transmutation. I intend to be alert and aware, to use the Violet Flame in each moment of need. I intend to live out loud, Divinely, with Spirit and joy as my constant companions, to notice the FUN aspect in all conditions and situations.

(Note—have pencil and paper handy.)

Beloved Friends! Let us energize ourselves. It is time to get down to business. We transmute the negative not only into the positive, but into the **glorious**.

Saint Germaine and the intense and holy Violet Flame transmute all which is placed into the vibrant Violet Flame from dark into light, into holy, into (re)new, into the radiant holy light of the Universe, of Spirit. *Place any energy into the Violet Flame, and the energy is transmuted and transformed. The transformed energy emerges as Divinely radiant, Divinely clear, Divinely loving energy, returned to the Universe.*

Find your sacred space and relax. *Let's have some fun and get business done.* Accomplishment and FUN are not mutually exclusive. Accomplishment and FUN are spiritual buddies.

Begin the Holy breath. In through the nose, out through the mouth. Breathe deeply.

Saint Germaine, I call you forth, with the Violet Flame of Transmutation. Be very alert to continuing the Holy Breath.

Consider the most vivid violet color you have ever seen, perhaps in a jewel or a flower petal, and hold the radiant image. The shimmering Violet Flame of Transmutation, placed safely and conveniently before you by Saint Germaine, is more beautiful, more vibrant, more glorious. Saint Germaine and the Violet Flame are your traveling companions as well, responding to you in any moment of need, simply with your breath and invitation.

Continue the Holy Breath. Think of an aspect of your life which you are having difficulty letting go of; an aspect which is "in your face". Perhaps an argument or anger in progress, a love affair, a grudge, a belief in your own unworthiness, or a pervading sense of hopelessness or lack of focus or direction. The list is infinite for the human condition.

This is the part we love. Let's have some fun, particularly where you are hard pressed to believe there is anything but frustration, annoyance, sadness and distress.

Violet Flame of Transmutation

There is FUN in transmutation. How grand. Continue the Holy Breath. Begin, as you are breathing, to envision yourself in a tube of Purple Light, shimmering, radiant, deep and brilliant, created for you by Saint Germaine. Feel the warmth as the Purple Light showers upon you, surrounds you, streams down upon you. *You are radiant.*

Continue to breathe, and continue to feel yourself embraced, protected, beloved by Spirit and St. Germaine. As you relax into the Purple Light, continue to breathe.

Let's do an internal audit. Consider the aspects of your experience which intrude upon your joy, your abundance, your sense of a fulfilled life. With your permission, we consider both personal and global. Personal first.

Continue the Holy Breath. In the personal, make a list. We are not kidding. Write at least three (or more) energies (situations, habits, conditions, annoyances) from which you would like to be free, which you choose to transmute into Divine love and Divine light.

Let's start with an energy/issue which you know does not serve you, but which you do not seem to be able to release, from the perspective of an act of will. Let=s use the example of a grudge.

Continue the Holy Breath. As an example, let us say you have a perception or belief that you have been wronged, terribly wronged. You *carry* the grudge.

You would like to have this horrendous weight removed, this destructive negativity pushing you down, harmfully influencing the quality of your life, your choices and your behavior.

You are being held back, rooted, shoes and feet, in messy, muddy gunk. How to get out of this place of seeming stuck? Place the experience and all related feelings, in all four bodies, into the Violet Flame of Transmutation.

Transmuting is easier than you think. Not an act of will, but an act of faith. You authentically offer and allow. Notice the results!

Continue the Holy Breath, and continue to envision yourself in the tube of Purple Light. We are not suggesting wishing away, "getting over it" or dismissing. Keep breathing! Experience what you are thinking and feeling.

Continue the Holy Breath. Turn your focus to transmuting each issue with the Violet Flame. Envision the Violet Flame before you, radiant, large. *Breathe in Spirit. Breathe!*

For example: I take this grudge and I place (breathe) it into the Holy Violet Flame of Transmutation. Envision the angry energy of the grudge being consumed by the brilliant Violet Flame, entering as a dark, cloudy form, and emerging as brilliant white energies of Divine light, Divine love.

Continue to breathe, beloveds. Go down the list. Release and transmute, one at a time. Breathe in God. Breathe out the negative energy, the experience, into the Violet Flame, to be transmuted, transformed and returned by the Divine as Holy, pure energies on the planet. Take as many breaths and as much time as you need with the Violet Flame.

Continue the Holy Breath. Look how you lighten your planet's energies each time you place something into the Violet Flame of Transmutation, into Divine love and Divine light!

Let us turn to troubling global issues. Beloved friends, let us place *the energies which produce* the issues into the Violet Flame of Transmutation.

What are the energies which produce war, racism, the waste and destruction of the precious planet upon which we live? At any moment, call forth the Violet Flame of Transmutation, perhaps even as you watch the news.

Return to the Holy Breath. I place the energies which contribute to (for example) war into the Violet Flame of

Transmutation. Breathe Spirit in. Breathe energies out. Dark or negative energies enter the Violet Flame and are transmuted. Vibrant, Divine energies of love and light emerge!

There is more power here than you imagine, beloveds, and we encourage you to place any energies which come into your awareness, your consciousness, into the Violet Flame of Transmutation.

A breath, an invitation, a brief moment—that's all you need to bring Saint Germaine and the Violet Flame into your presence, instantly.

Staff meetings at work, parent teacher conferences, encounters with children and spouse: as encounters occur, call forth Saint Germaine, the Violet Flame, and place the energies into the Violet Flame.

Get the job done in moments! Behold the Divine results, the Divine lightening and lifting!

Closing Affirmation
I AM wide awake and alert to notice any negative energies and immediately call forth the Holy Breath, Saint Germaine and the Violet Flame.
I AM liberated from holding any energies which do not serve.

Closing Prayer
Thank you for the blessing of an attitude of gratitude for all the many Divine gifts which I receive, and for my own Divine self. I intend to be very aware of each energy I experience, and **instantly** *with a breath, a thought and a prayer to call You, Saint Germaine, and the Violet Flame forward, that I may place the energies into the Violet Flame. For my liberation from trudging under the weight of old baggage, I thank you. For my joy and reawakening to FUN, I thank you. I intend to breathe in joy and Divine energies, and to breathe out other energies holding me*

back into the Violet Flame. I intend also to work towards a more global view and consciousness. Help me discern opportunities to best serve my self in all four bodies and our global community with the Violet Flame and the Holy Breath.

Author's note: In my own experience, I was much challenged to consider the energies I was placing into the Violet Flame without getting stuck or starting to stew about the issues at hand. Restarting with the Holy Breath helped me by breathing in Spirit and breathing out the energies for transmutation. I found it helpful, circumstances permitting, to have a violet candle or candleholder to ignite the image of the Violet Flame.

Chapter Three

Pink Ray of Unconditional Love, Wisdom, and Comfort
Mother Mary, Queen of Angels

The time is now. There is no "better" moment. Integrated within the Pink Ray are many energies, including hope, faith, courage, and the release of fears.

Opening Affirmation
Special I AM. Extraordinary in the Universe, I AM. Beloved in every moment, I AM. Free from fear, I AM.

Opening Prayer
In my spiritual, physical, mental and emotional life, in this moment, I seek Divine Unconditional Love, Wisdom and Comfort. I seek to rest, be refreshed and rejuvenated in the arms of Spirit. I ask to be bathed, within and without, with the Pink Light of Mother Mary, to experience Her healing energies. Within the safety and strength of the Pink Radiance, I ask the Divine to help me release my fears. I thank the Divine and Mother Mary for this precious time of healing and enjoyment, which I so freely and eagerly embrace.

Invitation and Permission
I invite Mother Mary and the Pink Ray of Unconditional Love, Wisdom and Comfort into my heart, my soul, and all four bodies. I give my permission to fully allow Mother Mary to direct the Pink Ray to any part of all four bodies where it is most needed.

I allow the Divine Pink Light to reawaken the DNA in my physical body.

From Mother Mary: *Welcome, my beloveds, to this time of healing. Even as the Pink Ray of Unconditional Love, Wisdom and Comfort surrounds and heals you, I love and embrace you, and offer my healing energies.*
*My beloveds, the time is **now**. There is no later time which is more convenient, more appropriate, more "enlightened," or otherwise "better" than this moment. I AM here, my beloveds. Your I AM is here also.*
Let us launch this brilliant journey, this radiant healing, together. You may wonder: what have I to gain from this healing and meditation? First, be reminded of how truly beloved and extraordinary you are in the Divine.
Gain your freedom and liberation from fear. Trust me with your fears, including the "I'm not good enough and I'm not getting this right" fear. The unconditional love offered to you by Spirit and the Pink Ray of Unconditional Love, Wisdom and Comfort leaves no room for fear; only for Divine unconditional love and truth. Therein lives comfort—in your recognition of who you truly are!

Seek your sacred space. Begin the Holy Breath. Invite, into your heart center, Mother Mary and the Pink Ray of Unconditional Love, Wisdom and Comfort.

Continue to breathe. The Pink Light begins to warm the heart area, resting, moving through the heart, radiating. Continue to breathe in the holy energies of the Pink Ray of Unconditional Love, Wisdom and Comfort.

Perhaps you may feel a sense of fluttering in your heart, or tingling in your fingertips. Whether you experience the flutters or not, Mother Mary is lovingly with you.

Continue the Holy Breath. Those areas of your heart, tired, exhausted by disappointment, distress, fear, the illusion of unworthiness and not being "good enough," awaken to the rejuvenation, *even to exaltation* as the Pink Ray of Unconditional Love, Wisdom and Comfort brightens each tired cell, awakening the very DNA strands, with the subtle fragrance of sweet roses.

Each DNA strand is enveloped and regenerated by the rose fragrance and the intense Pink Light. Comfort and peace are reawakened and re-established.

Beloveds, continue the Holy Breath. Pause, especially as you focus the Pink Ray in your heart. Where Divine love abides, there is no room for fear, doubt, despair, or rage. In your heart, with the Pink Ray, create room only for love of self and others.

Continue the Holy Breath. The Pink Ray seeks every corner of your heart. Envision the flowing Pink Light, this shower of rose petals, radiant and Pink, replacing the dark spaces with the fragrance of roses and Pink Light, one clouded space at a time.

Where Divine love abides, hope replaces despair.
Where Divine love abides, love replaces fear.
Where Divine love abides, strength replaces doubt.
Certainty, faith and clarity reside.

Divine, unconditional love replaces all which does not serve. I AM beautiful, as the most beautiful rose. I AM worthy. I AM Divinely loved. I AM extraordinary. I AM part of the ONE.

Continue to breathe. Mother Mary and the Pink Ray of Unconditional Love, Wisdom and Comfort continue to seek each corner of your heart: healing, radiating, revealing, reawakening comfort and wisdom, so much a part of Divine unconditional love.

Your hands begin to tingle with the radiance, comfort, power and energies of the Pink Light of Mother Mary. Continue the Holy Breath.

The Pink Ray, expanding and radiating, penetrates and surrounds every part of your heart, your head, your brain, so you may think with love, and live your life with Divine unconditional love, wisdom and comfort.

The Pink Light penetrates and surrounds every part of your ears, that you hear and *listen* with Divine unconditional love, wisdom, and comfort.

Continue the Holy Breath. The Pink Ray of Unconditional Love surrounds and penetrates your eyes. In this and future moments, your eyes watch, see and reflect Divine unconditional love, wisdom, and comfort.

Continue the Holy Breath. The loving Pink Ray infuses and surrounds every part of your mouth and throat, that you *speak and intone* with Divine unconditional love, wisdom, and comfort.

The Pink Ray continues to expand into the arms, where love and compassion are embraced freely, held freely, given freely, ever replenished, ever present. Continue the Holy Breath. Uplift your self and others with each movement of hands and arms.

Radiating throughout the body, the Pink Ray penetrates every organ, every function, every movement, down to the feet, where every step is a Divine step of love, for self, for others.

Continue the Holy Breath. Thank You, Spirit. Thank You, Mother Mary, for the Pink Ray of Divine Unconditional Love, Wisdom and Comfort.

Pink Ray and the Release of Fears

Continue the Holy Breath. Feel the Pink Radiance of unconditional love penetrate every particle of your being, in all four bodies: mental, physical, spiritual, and emotional. Each of your four bodies is radiant, glistening with the Divine, unconditional love of Mother Mary and the Pink Ray of Love, Wisdom and Comfort.

You are safely enveloped in Divine, unconditional love and powerful protection with the Pink Ray, flowing through you.

Continue to breathe. Consider your fears. Within the radiant energies of the Pink Ray, embrace your fears, one at a time. It may be easier to start with the lesser, and work up to the greater and larger fears.

Continue the Holy Breath. Within this love, summon the first fear. Acknowledge the fear, thank it, love the fear. Recognize the limitation the fear may have placed upon and within you.

Continue the Holy Breath. The radiance of the Pink Ray of Unconditional Love, Wisdom and Comfort continues to shimmer and emanate within you, to love you and to love the fear. Release the fear to Spirit. Continue the process as much as you are able in this moment. Return to the meditation as often as you choose.

Mother Mary's healing energies remain with you, in this and all moments.

Closing Affirmation
Fearless I am to live my life fully. Holy I AM. Wise and loving, I AM. Divine comfort I offer, Divine comfort I AM.

Closing Prayer
As I see roses, enjoy their fragrance, I AM reminded of Divine unconditional love, radiance, and compassion of Mother Mary's Pink Ray within me, of Her Divine love for me. Help me, Spirit, to notice my own Divine value, to be reminded of the Divine-ness within me, to live and express, to myself and others, the Divine comfort, wisdom and compassion I have so freely received, in every breath. I call upon my own Divine wisdom, to hand my fears over to Spirit, to live a more liberated, loving life.

Author's note: I felt The Pink Ray arrive with great warmth in my heart area, and I could feel the Pink Light spreading and radiating. I experienced flutters in the heart, fingers tingling, which subsided somewhat as the meditation continued, replaced by a general sense of warmth. I sensed Mother Mary's energies enfolding me, around my shoulders, Her chin gently resting on my shoulder. Mother Mary's energies for me are very powerful, very warm, very embracing, very fun.

Chapter Four

Brilliant Pink Ray of Forgiveness and Absolution
Lady Quan Yin, Divine Goddess of Mercy, Compassion and Charity

Forgive Divinely, to liberate yourself.

Opening Affirmation
*Holy I AM. Worthy I AM. For**given** I AM. For**giving** I AM. Liberated I AM.*

Opening Prayer
Lady Quan Yin, I invite you and the Brilliant Pink Ray of Forgiveness and Absolution that I may experience the Divine gift of Divine forgiveness within me. Lift the burdens weighing upon my heart and soul. I accept the gift of Divine forgiveness, indwelling within my heart and soul. I intend to Divinely forgive myself and others in Spirit, that which seems impossible to forgive in this worldly arena. With Spirit's love, I Divinely forgive myself and others lovingly. I bless and release—I absolve—my own self and others into liberation and freedom to move forward upon the lighted path.

Invitation and Permission
I invite Lady Quan Yin and the Brilliant Pink Ray of Forgiveness and Absolution into my heart, my soul, and all four bodies. I give my permission to fully allow Lady Quan Yin to direct the Brilliant Pink Ray to any part of all four bodies where it is most needed.

I allow the Brilliant Pink Ray to reawaken the DNA in my physical body.

Let us begin, beloveds, with the *forgiveness of self and others.* Forgiveness can not be offered or "achieved" by purposeful will. The Divine self allows and offers forgiveness where the emotional and intellectual bodies are not able to forgive. *Forgiveness is the expression of Divine unconditional love and a Divine state of grace.*

The energy of absolution is the bestowing upon yourself, or upon another, the Divine energies of pardon, release, liberation and freedom. With absolution, you actively release that which is imprisoning and burdening you, holding you back. *When you offer absolution to self or another, you in turn liberate yourself.*

Find or create your sacred space. Begin the Holy Breath. Envision the Brilliant Pink Ray of Lady Quan Yin as "hot pink," the brilliant pink color sometimes seen in sunsets.

Know you are worthy to receive Divine forgiveness and healing, to Divinely forgive and offer absolution (liberation) for *yourself and others.*

When forgiveness seems or feels impossible in each of the four bodies, it may indeed be impossible within the human condition. *Divine forgiveness*, not only possible for the *Divine self*, is Divinely assured.

Let's take care of the home front first: forgiveness and absolution of self, with the forgiveness of others following. *Lady Quan Yin, I invite you and the Brilliant Pink Ray encompassing your loving energies of Divine forgiveness and absolution (freedom, release, liberation) into my heart center.*

Notice the Brilliant Pink Ray warmth in your upper back, feel yourself being elevated, as Lady Quan Yin's energies enter surround and enfold you. As always, beloveds, Her gentleness

Brilliant Pink Ray of FORGIVENESS and Absolution

and intense, laser like power merge to serve your healing. *Divinely for**giving** I AM. Divinely for**given** I AM.*

Let us relieve the *self* of personal grudges and *I should and should not haves*, encumbering our present and future, holding us in terrible and weighty limitation. Our energies, our lives are imprisoned and held hostage by guilt and lack of forgiveness of our own selves.

Breathe the Holy Breath. The Brilliant Pink Ray *is* Divine forgiveness. *Forgiveness and absolution of self, in my physical, mental, emotional and spiritual bodies, I offer, I receive and I accept as a Divine gift to myself.*

Continue to breathe as the Brilliant Pink Ray expands, moving across your shoulders, towards your head. The Brilliant Pink Light rests there, seeking those places where grudges against self and others are held, releasing, reawakening each DNA fiber with the Brilliant Pink Ray of Forgiveness and Absolution.

It is the Divine Self which forgives, not the human condition. With Brilliant Pink light within you, Divinely forgive yourself as the Brilliant Pink Ray lovingly, individually washes away self recrimination in each DNA fiber.

Continue the Holy Breath. Continue to feel the Brilliant Pink Ray healing each area of the brain where you have stored grudges and convictions against yourself, consciously or inadvertently.

I Divinely forgive myself. I allow the Divine compassion and Divine unconditional love of Lady Quan Yin and the Brilliant Pink Ray to continue to heal me. I accept the healing of Divine forgiveness. I AM Divine forgiveness.

DNA is not consumed. Instead, the Brilliant Pink Light envelops and resurrects each DNA strand with love, allowing the love and light of the Brilliant Pink Ray to transform and heal with Divine forgiveness.

The Brilliant Pink Ray searches, bathes, heals, rests, and moves on, seeking the places where grudges and angers have been harboring and hiding for years.

The thoughts and emotions of wrongdoing against self or others may surface as the Brilliant Pink Ray lights the dark spots for healing—a neon flash, gentle, strong, heals the energies which have been preventing forgiveness, including malice, resentment, self righteousness, or indignation.

Each of these individual grudges is keeping a part of your "self" in a prison. It is the mission of the Brilliant Pink Ray to seek each "prison cell" and unlock it with love and devotion. As the healing of forgiveness occurs, the Brilliant Pink Ray presents the other aspect and gift of forgiveness: absolution, liberty, pardon, freedom.

Continue the Holy Breath. The Brilliant Pink Ray continues to seek those dark, heavy areas where the cells are living in self recrimination: regret, resentment of self and guilt. Let us not judge the situations, life episodes, experiences and decisions from which the self-condemnation arose; rather we seek to release the guilt and offer ourselves the Divine gift of forgiveness and absolution. Lady Quan Yin lovingly continues to guide the Brilliant Pink Ray for the forgiveness of self.

You may initially experience some attachment in the mental and emotional bodies, by habit and intensity, to the belief in personal guilt and wrongdoing.

Love your resistance and Divinely forgive yourself. Thank you, resistance, and I accept the healing of forgiveness and absolution of myself.

Holy I AM. Worthy I AM. Forgiving I AM. Forgiven I AM. Absolved I AM.

Forgiveness of others

Once the self is Divinely forgiven, we move forward to Divinely forgive others. Continue the Holy Breath. *Forgiveness and absolution of others **I offer as a gift** to my self and others. Forgiveness and absolution of others **I receive and accept as a gift** to myself and others.*

The Brilliant Pink Ray knows where the grudges, rages, angers and resentments against others are harboring in the darkness.

Continue the Holy Breath. Lady Quan Yin is reviving the Brilliant Pink Ray energies. Once again, allow the Brilliant Pink Ray to tour the body, lighten, enlighten and absolve (liberate, pardon) the grudges against others, replacing negative emotions and energies with the unconditional light and love of Divine forgiveness.

You *do not need to approve of, or justify*, the actions of others (or self) to forgive. You only need to *allow* the Brilliant Pink Ray to (re)awaken Divine love and Divine forgiveness within your heart.

Breathe in the Holy Breath. Allow the Brilliant Pink Ray to survey and envelop, in Divine forgiveness and love, your DNA cells holding angers and grudges against others.

Continue the Holy Breath. The Brilliant Pink Ray once again tours the body, resting in each cell where guilt, resentment and anger have harbored.

With Lady Quan Yin's direction, the Brilliant Pink Ray shapes almost as a key to unlock the treasure of life and light within the darkness, pausing, lighting, unlocking, lifting to the light, lightening the weight, healing, moving on.

In this way, Lady Quan Yin's energies and the Brilliant Pink Ray moves through the body, enveloping each cell and DNA fiber with love, forgiveness and absolution, gently *washing each* grudge, *with light,* especially, in the head and heart.

The Brilliant Pink Ray continues to move throughout the body. Once more, you may perhaps experience attachment to the energies of "having been wronged." You have already Divinely released much resistance towards healing and forgiveness of self.

Divinely release your resistance once again towards forgiveness of others: love your resistance, forgive, absolve. Thank you, resistance; thank you, attachment to habit. As I accepted my own Divine forgiveness of self, I now allow Divine forgiveness and absolution of others. All four of your bodies—mental, emotional, physical and spiritual, have been healed in forgiveness and absolution of self and others. You are lighter and more free.

Closing Affirmation
I AM of Spirit. I AM Divine. I AM Divine Forgiveness, towards my self and others. I AM liberated and absolved.

Closing Prayer
Into my consciousness, my very soul, help me to discern my own bright light and truth. I AM a spark of the Divine, and the Divine is within me. I release to the Holy Light my human need and attachment, in the mental, intellectual, emotional and physical bodies, to reason out or to force myself to try to forgive myself or others. With the help of Spirit, with the healings of Lady Quan Yin and the Brilliant Pink Ray, I offer Divine forgiveness and absolution to my self, and to others, in the abundant, unconditional love of Spirit.

Author's note: I experienced a real sense of the energies of Lady Quan Yin coming in from behind, with warmth from the right side. I felt butterflies in the heart area as the Brilliant Pink Ray rested and healed there, and my fingertips tingled. As the healing became more complete, I experienced a sense of rest, and the butterflies were replaced with a sense of being enveloped in a warm, soothing mist.

Chapter Five

Mauve Ray: Clarity of Intention
Archangel Uriel,
Archangel of Transformation

Intentionality!
Clarity of intention is essential, in order
to manifest with Spirit.
Rather than change similar for similar,
we transform old to new and better.
Change is not enough. Transformation is required.

Opening Affirmation
Divine I AM. I express Divinely. I AM ready and willing to transform. I AM ready and willing to create and state clear intentions, to inform Spirit and the Universe of my intentions. I expect miraculous, Divine manifestation of my intentions.

Opening Prayer
I offer this prayer of my willingness and intention to transform my reality on all levels; to allow perfect, unlimited clarity of intention, in order to co-create with the Divine. I AM willing and I AM ready, with crystal clear clarity, to listen to Divine guidance and enjoy Divine miracles.

Invitation and Permission
I invite Archangel Uriel and the Mauve Ray for Clarity of Intention into my heart, my soul, and all four bodies. I give my

permission to fully allow Archangel Uriel to direct the Mauve Light to any part of all four bodies where it is most needed. I allow the Mauve Light to reawaken the DNA in my physical body.

Beloveds: let us focus on the clarity of intention. *It is truly essential for you to be **clear** about what you want, need, and desire, in order to inform Spirit and the Universe. You must have clarity of intention in order to manifest the co-created miracles.* Change is not enough. Transformation is required. Spirit is standing by to assist and inspire you in every moment. Archangel Uriel, Archangel of Transformation, awaits your invitation.

Pick an area of your life where you want to create a change—a transformation. You know that you wish a change, but consider: what exactly is that change?

Clarity of intention helps you to discern and choose: same for same, or let go of past patterns and embrace the new, more beneficial and exciting.

Be aware of what you intend, because your intention is what manifests.

We can change or move from one point to another, yet remain relatively the same. With clarity of intention, we *transform*. We transform *any* situation or condition, whether personal, professional or financial—from where we are, to a new level: to a forward, deeper, higher plane, new, more vibrant, and more beneficial. We do not necessarily trade like for like.

Cloudy intentions bring cloudy results. Clear intentions clearly manifest clear manifestations. *Go for the clear and miraculous intention, to bring about miraculous results.*

Let us use an example of a relationship. Perhaps you have recently parted with someone, and you might be feeling empty and frustrated. "This always happens to me," you say to your friends. "I seem to attract the same type all the time." Soon, you may begin to seek a new relationship, but perhaps with the same old patterns.

Examine your intention, beloveds. In your heart, do you long for a new relationship? What is your real intention? Do you intend to be valued, treasured and cherished? Would you rather be considered as pleasant and convenient?

Do you intend to have someone in your life who you admire, enjoy and are delighted to be with, or, by default, content to have someone you don't mind being with?

You can see beloveds, that there is a great deal of difference in these intentions. Be clear about what you intend. To discover and create our true intentions, to inform Spirit and the Universe, Archangel Uriel is offering us the gift of the Mauve Ray for Clarity of Intention.

Out loud, state your intention! Write it down! Inform Spirit! Inform the Universe! Your clear intention must be stated to manifest the results.

Seek your sacred space of stillness, with no interruptions. Begin the Holy Breath. If you are away, and discover the need to clarify your intention when and where you are, create your sacred space in a moment with your Holy Breath. Archangel Uriel awaits your invitation, and is with you immediately, what ever your circumstance.

Breathe deeply. If you have trouble focusing, close your eyes and count your breaths. If you have a distracting thought, simply take another breath and begin again.

Archangel Uriel, I invite you and the Mauve Ray for Clarity of Intention, to help me discern, create and state my true, clear intention, and be fully present with my own clarity of intention. With the Mauve Ray, I manifest with my Divine partners: transformation, my clear intentions, leaving the old behind, moving into the new.

Continue the Holy Breath. *I AM worthy to create my clarity of intention. I intend goodness and abundance in all experiences and interactions. I AM worthy to intend my heart's true desire.*

Archangel Uriel is at this moment enveloping you in his wings, bringing to you the Mauve Ray for Clarity of Intention.

Feel the warmth of the Mauve Ray and Archangel Uriel's energies on your upper right side, expanding radiantly towards your head.

Continue the Holy Breath. The Mauve Ray, like a traveling microscope or a body scan, seeks out doubt, fear, belief in obstacles, limitations, the illusion of unworthiness, and transforms, transforms, transforms.

Continue the Holy Breath. With your breath, the Mauve Ray radiates through you—resting and healing each molecule, each cell, physically reawakening each DNA strand, transforming the belief in limitation into the availability for limitless, miraculous intentions and results.

The Mauve Ray transforms in order for you to discover and create your true, heartfelt intention.

Continue the Holy Breath.

As the Mauve Ray moves through you, breathe in. Experience the Mauve Light revealing and transforming beliefs, fear and doubt. The Mauve Ray continues now, expanding into the heart, healing, transforming.

Continue the Holy Breath.

The Mauve Light continues to glow, radiant throughout your entire being, in all four bodies, transforming, healing. Your DNA cells are revived, transformed, reawakened to the desires of your heart and soul.

The shimmering Mauve Ray continues to seek all limiting beliefs which have been holding you back, transforming each old belief into new, unlimited abundance.

Distill, as you would distill essences from flowers, the purest clarity of your desires and intentions. The Mauve Ray embraces and enhances these clear intentions, freeing energies of limitation, helping you to even further clarify in order to manifest.

Archangel Uriel continues to direct the Mauve Ray. Rest, relax, enjoy the energies.

Remember, beloveds: state out loud, and write down each intention. Offer the intention, with perfect clarity, to the Universe, to Spirit, to yourself. You are Co-creator of miracles as you inform Spirit and the Universe of your intentions.

Be alert and aware! Watch for the miracles. Write down the manifestation of each intention—the miracles—as each occur. Clarity of intention equals divine manifestation.

Enjoy and continue to do this meditation. The more practice you have in allowing and stating clarity of intention, the more Co-created Divine miracles you manifest!

Closing Affirmation

Holy I AM. With perfect clarity, I offer my intentions to the Universe and await the miracles. Vigilant, thankful and aware to notice the Divine, miraculous manifestations, I AM.

Closing Prayer

Precious Spirit, thank you for my clarity of intention, that I may manifest my heart's true desire. I intend to use the clarity of intention for my highest good, for humanity and all living things on this Earth, which is my home. I also intend to be exceptionally aware of the manifestation of the Divine miracles which result from my intentions. I realize the miracles are an expression of Your unconditional Divine Love, of our Divine connection, and I AM ever thankful.

Author's note: I felt the energies of Archangel Uriel come in from the back, upper body, from the right side, and expand. Almost immediately I could feel my heart area pulsing and fingertips tingle. The warmth of the energies seem to continue in the heart area after the meditation was complete.

Chapter Six

Yellow Ray: Reactivation of Joy
Archangel Jo(y)phiel,
Archangel of Illumination

Joy is not a condition we seek.
Joy is an experience we allow.

Opening Affirmation
Joy I AM. Joy I offer. Joy I express. Joy I receive.
I AM Joy-full.

Opening Prayer
Archangel Jophiel, uplift my heart that I may know my own joy. I offer my trust and faith, my very joy, to be reawakened, resurrected. Uncover, reactivate my joy. I intend to be joy-full, to offer and receive my joy. Open my awareness to the value of joy, and opportunities to express my joy and to have fun. I intend my joy to radiate and uplift those around me.

Invitation and Permission
I invite Archangel Jophiel and the Yellow Ray for the Reactivation of Joy into my heart, my soul, and all four bodies. I give my permission to fully allow Archangel Jophiel to direct the Yellow Light to any part of all four bodies where it is most needed. I allow the Yellow Light to reawaken the DNA in my physical body.

Archangel Jophiel (Jo(y)phiel) would like you to be aware that your joy does not depend upon others around you, or on your external circumstances.

I AM my joy. Joy is a form of faith. When we resurrect and reawaken joy, we resurrect and reawaken a deeper faith, a confidence in the Divine.

The Yellow Ray for the Reactivation of Joy is gentle, yet very powerful. Envision the brilliant yellow rays of the sun. You can enjoy and experience the penetrating warmth of the sun's rays, yet their radiance is too bright to behold with your eyes. Such is the brilliant Yellow Ray of Joy. Let's have some fun.

Perhaps you feel that there is too much to do to take time out for a little fun, or perhaps it seems that the "joy has gone out" of life.

All you need is a little refresher course, some reactivation, and a spark of re-ignition of the joy you have indwelling.

You never lose your joy, although your joy may feel asleep or deactivated between the "I wish I had/had not", "I should/should have/should not have".

The Yellow Ray *reawakens that which already is*—polishing and refurbishing your every cell, your DNA!

Do you feel some joy, but also feel the doldrums/*dull-drums*? The Yellow Ray transforms this so-so condition and opens your being *fully* to the fun and joy *which Spirit intends for you and of which you are indeed worthy.* **Joy is important in your lives, beloveds—don't underestimate the value of joy, the vitality which is joy, and the energies of having fun!**

We begin. Seek your sacred space. Begin the Holy Breath. Each breath re-oxygenates each cell, moving the healing process—the resurrection and reawakening process—forward. Keep drinking water handy.

As we begin, consider a brilliant yellow image—perhaps the radiant sun, a brilliant yellow bouquet of flowers, or a personal object or image of your own representing warm, brilliant yellow.

Yellow Ray: Reactivation of Joy

Continue the Holy Breath. No matter if you become distracted. Just begin with again with a new breath.

Archangel Jophiel, I invite you and the Yellow Ray to reactivate my joy. Immediately, Archangel Jophiel is surrounding you, smiling, beaming, enveloping you with Divine love.

Breathe in the warmth, feel the brilliance of the streaming, brilliant Yellow Ray.

Imagine feeling chilly, coming in from icy weather, and basking in a warm, cozy corner of your home. Feel yourself absorbing and enjoying the toasty, healing rays of the bright sun streaming in through your window. This is your own personal thawing out. Shake off the icy sense of indifference and the illusion of unworthiness! Absorb and experience the warmth of unconditional love!

Breathe out the chill. Continue to breathe in the warmth of the Yellow Ray. Powerful, warm, enveloping and relaxing.

Continue the Holy Breath. Breathe in the Yellow Light, breathe out the chill. With each breath, you continue to reignite, resurrect, reawaken your joy in each cell.

Yellow Ray, warm, infuse, envelop, and enfold me with your Light.

Every cell, every part of you, in all four bodies, is being infused with the Light.

Archangel Jophiel, in Your radiance I am wrapped. The chill of indifference and the illusion of unworthiness is melted away by the Yellow Ray of Joy.

Absorb the Yellow Ray with every pore of your body. Absorb its warmth. Imagine that you are sitting before the sun, and the sun is warming your back.

The Yellow Ray is penetrating at this moment, seeking, discovering and reactivating, reawakening your DNA of joy.

Yellow ray move through me. With spectacular flair, I fling open those areas of my mental, physical, emotional and spiritual bodies, previously closed to joy, to be revitalized by the warmth of the Yellow Radiance.

Continue to breathe. With each breath, joy is reignited in each of your cells. *My joy is reawakening.*

The Yellow Ray continues to spread its warmth, in through the back, permeating, warming through each of your pores.

The seeds of joy are planted in the heart at the moment of birth. The seeds may be nurtured and blossom in a great, continuing harvest, or perhaps be trampled upon, suppressing the seeds and the blossoms.

These seeds of joy reside within your DNA. The disheartened seeds of joy remain dormant, eagerly thirsting for Archangel Jophiel Yellow Ray. The DNA seeds of joy, receiving streams of brilliant Yellow Light, directed by Archangel Jophiel, arise to life, spreading, shining, propagating joy in all four bodies and to all those nearby.

All conditions are loved by the Yellow Ray, which seeks each DNA strand of joy to enhance, reawaken, reactivate, resurrect.

Bask, shine, feel the Yellow Light move through you. Continue to breathe.

Envision the warm Yellow Ray reawakening, resurrecting each DNA strand of joy.

The already joyful strands are made more joyful with the Yellow Ray tickling, enhancing, and resurrecting even a deeper joy. The awaiting DNA strands are awakening to their own truth—their own joy.

Affirm: *I AM Joyful. I AM Holy. I AM Worthy. I AM God.*

Reunited with your joy you are. Holy you are. Joyful you are. Affirm: *Reunited with my joy I AM. Holy I AM. Joyful I AM.* Continue to breathe.

Joy is not an experience you seek—rather joy is a condition which you allow. Always we hear: I want to be happy, I want to have joy in my life. We offer to you—look around your self, your environment, the people around you who stir your heart. Notice and be aware.

Invite Archangel Jophiel and the Yellow Ray of Joy into your heart, mind, body and soul at *any moment*! A quick refresher course is always available, always welcome!

Remember to **allow** joy. *Joy I AM. Joy I manifest.* There is, in fact, joy in every moment. Joy can not be forced, only allowed. Allow joy, notice joy.

Joy replaces dismay, anger, and frustration. Archangel Jophiel is imprinting the Yellow Ray upon you, responding to your invitation, in spectacular abundance and beauty. As the Yellow Ray moves through you, your ability to perceive and experience joy in all conditions and situations is resurrected.

So be it. So joy is. Joy is in your being—your joy is ignited and active, joy expressing and joy ready to express.

Archangel Jo(y)phiel, ready in any moment serve you, awaits your next invitation.

Closing Affirmation
My being, in all four bodies, is reunited with my Divine joy.
My joy is reactivated, resurrected, reawakened.

Closing Prayer
Beloved Spirit, thank you for the Joy I AM, and for the Faith I AM. I intend to be aware of the joy within me as I behold the brilliant yellows of this Universe. I intend to notice and be aware the joy within me each time I feel the warmth of the sun. I pray for my continued awareness of my own joy and my own faith. Thank You for the reunion of joy and faith and the resurrection of joy within me.

Author's note: I felt the warmth of the Yellow Ray absorbing from behind me, starting on the right side, through my back, with my fingers tingling. Using the image of the sun's warmth enveloping me, and feeling warmth penetrate following a chill, is very helpful to me in this meditation. Offered as gifts to us by Archangel Jophiel, this "sun image" and the image of brilliant yellow blossoming flowers inspired me. Often, as I enjoy yellow flowers, I think of the joy which resides within me.

Chapter Seven

Turquoise Ray of Tranquility
Find Tranquility in the Midst of Inner and Outer Turmoil
Archangel Zoriah,
Archangel of the Brilliant Rainbow

Divinity in, turmoil out.
Unnecessary to struggle in the storm raging around you.
Find rest in the Oasis of Peace and Tranquility.

Opening Affirmation
Peace I AM. Clarity and Divine perspective I AM.
In the face of it all,
Divine tranquility I AM.

Opening Prayer
In this and any moment of turmoil, keep me mindful and confident of my spiritual tools. I ask for Divine guidance to envision myself bathed in a cascade of shimmering, radiant Turquoise Light, with Archangel Zoriah enfolding me. Help me to be fully present, with full Divine recognition: I AM an oasis of tranquility, completely independent of the emotions and conditions of others. Divinely guide me, especially when I am engulfed by turmoil and anxiety, within and without, to be faithful, notice and be mindful of all Divine healing available in simple breath and a prayer, wherever I am, whomever I am near, and whatever I am doing, in all circumstances.

Invitation and Permission

I invite Archangel Zoriah and the Turquoise Ray of Tranquility into my heart, my soul, and all four bodies. I give my permission to fully allow Archangel Zoriah to direct the Turquoise Ray to any part of all four bodies where it is most needed. I allow the Turquoise Light to reawaken the DNA in my physical body.

There are times; it seems to each of us, that we are drowning in the churning worlds of outer and inner turmoil. Nothing short of Divine intervention is needed to achieve *or allow* a state of inner tranquility—that we might catch our spiritual, mental, emotional and even physical breath.

The peace and tranquility which we seek, so elusive in our immediate world, *is ours simply for the invitation to Spirit* to bring it forth in our lives.

Archangel Zoriah, Archangel of the Brilliant Rainbow, stands poised, arms outstretched, awaiting your invitation for the Turquoise Ray of Tranquility to serve you. With His Turquoise Light, Archangel Zoriah creates the oasis of peace and balance in your physical, mental, emotional and spiritual bodies, so deeply needed and desired.

Archangel Zoriah wants you to know: *wherever you are, whatever your circumstances, internal or external, you need not be in turmoil. I AM with you in a thought, in a moment, a breath. My arms are open to enfold you. Call me forth. I await your invitation.*

Tranquility is not a passive energy or space—it is a peaceful, vital energy and space which allows you to pause, to move into and receive positive energies and clarity, in the mental, emotional, physical and even spiritual bodies. Fear and turmoil may otherwise cloud or deny your Divine clarity and perspective.

For tranquility in the midst of turmoil, let us begin. Seek your sacred space. Begin the Holy Breath.

This meditation, beloveds, is often needed quickly, instantly, when you are out and about. Create your own sacred space, wherever you are, with the Holy Breath. Invite Archangel Zoriah with a thought and brief prayer. His response to you is instant.

Breathe in God. *I call forth Archangel Zoriah, Archangel of the Brilliant Rainbow, and the healing Turquoise Ray of Tranquility.*

Continue the Holy Breath. Envision your turmoil as a jagged, rocky terrain, from which you seek rescue and release.

You behold a breathtaking, brilliant, Divine rainbow of Blues and Greens, emanating Turquoise Light, above the jagged rocks on which you find yourself. Archangel Zoriah, taking your hand, helps you to easily step upon the Divine Rainbow, which transforms into your own personal Cloud of Light, radiating Divine Greens and Blues, a Turquoise Light and energy.

Continue the Holy Breath. Upon this cloud, you are transported to an oasis above the barren, jagged turmoil which surrounds you. The shimmering Greens and Blues of Divine, Liquid Light create an Oasis of Turquoise Light awaiting you. Gently, alight from the cloud of liquid Divine Blue and Green energies into the Archangel Zoriah's Oasis of Turquoise light, comforting, safe, tranquil.

Know yourself to be enfolded in Archangel Zoriah's wings, as you enjoy the Turquoise Light Oasis. The turmoil in all four bodies is already beginning to be healed by the Turquoise Light of Archangel Zoriah.

Breathe. As the meditation continues, Archangel Zoriah leads you to a path of Turquoise Light, shimmering around your feet. The Turquoise Light path comes into sharper focus as the Divine perspective brings clarity.

Within the space in which you find yourself, continue this Holy Breath. You are being filled with the Light of Spirit. When tranquility is allowed, discernment, clarity and the compassionate view naturally follow.

Turquoise Ray of tranquility, infuse your light within me.
Turquoise Ray of tranquility,
diffuse your light throughout me.
Turquoise Ray of tranquility,
create the Turquoise light radiant within me.

I open my heart and mind to the Turquoise Ray.
I open my soul to the Turquoise Ray.
I open my being to the Turquoise Ray.

Reactivate my DNA to remember Divine peace.
Reignite and restore my state of Divine tranquility.

Envision the Turquoise Ray of Tranquility within and around you, a shimmering, radiant, flow of energy, showering you with radiant Divine Light, cascading brilliantly with the energies of joy, peace and discernment. You are safe and protected by Spirit, by your angels, and by Archangel Zoriah. With your own unique spiritual seatbelt, designed by Archangel Zoriah, you are ready to zoom out of turmoil, into peace, and all of the gifts which peace brings.

As you continue the Holy Breath, feel your fingertips tingle with the Turquoise Ray as its warmth begins to enter your auric field—the field of energies around you—and your body.

As Turquoise energies enfold you, you may feel a powerful sense of expansion and heat from behind you, especially your upper back and behind your head.

The Turquoise Ray lights the brain and the brain stem. The rocky seas are being made tranquil as the Turquoise Ray infuses each of your DNA strands with Divine assurance and tranquility.

Each cell is blessed. Continue to breathe. Perhaps you may feel a sense of expansion across your shoulders and arms, down to your fingertips, as the Turquoise Ray of Tranquility continues to flow through you, with Archangel Zoriah's guidance. Continue the Holy Breath.

The Turquoise Ray is tracing, slowly down your spine, each cell, each nerve, each DNA fiber, bringing peace and tranquility. Continue to breathe. The Turquoise Ray pauses, and rests where needed.

The Turquoise Flow continues to expand, through each of your muscles, back, chest, heart area, solar plexus, pausing, resting as needed. You are infused with the radiant Turquoise Light.

The Turquoise flow of Light seeks the origins of your anxiety and turmoil, replacing them with peace and security.

The gentle showers of Turquoise Light discover and Divinely heal each seed and energy of dismay, distress, anxiety and turmoil, infusing Turquoise energies of Divine Tranquility, Divine light, Divine clarity, Divine perspective, and Divine unconditional love.

Divinity in, turmoil out and transformed.

Continue the Holy Breath. The Turquoise Ray continues to radiate all the way down to the soles of your feet, pausing, resting, infusing tranquility.

Archangel Zoriah does not seek to diminish or devalue the importance or severity of circumstances, inner or outer, in which you find yourself.

Rather, Archangel Zoriah and the Divine Tranquility energies place the circumstances in Divine perspective.

Within your own Divine perspective, anxiety and turmoil are released, replaced by Divine love and light, restoring clarity. Clarity and discernment restored, peace and balance return.

Continue to breathe as Archangel Zoriah and the shimmering Turquoise Flow do their holy work. As you breathe, the Turquoise Light calms and soothes the central nervous system, restoring balance. Continue to breathe. Balance is restored in all four bodies: mental, emotional, physical and spiritual.

Each step, in all four bodies, is blessed now. No more running, reacting, rebounding to and fro in any of your bodies. Your very steps, still guided by strength and courage, are now enacted with purpose, lighter, and more peaceful. Thank Archangel Zoriah. Thank Spirit. Your being is blessed in Divine grace and tranquility. Call upon Archangel Zoriah and the Turquoise Ray of Tranquility at any moment. With the Holy Breath, inhale Turquoise Light and turmoil is transformed into Divine tranquility.

Closing Affirmation
Free from turmoil I AM. Independent of the circumstances and emotions of others which surround me, I AM.
Present with the Divine, in an oasis of tranquility, in a breath, I AM.

Closing Prayer
I AM thankful to for my independence from any turmoil and chaos which surround me. I AM thankful for replacing turmoil and confusion with Divine discernment and clarity. I AM thankful for this oasis of peace, allowing me to hold the Divine perspective. I intend to be ever mindful of Divine guidance and gifts offered and available to me; of Archangel Zoriah's readiness to enfold me within the light of the Turquoise Ray of Tranquility. Help me also to be mindful that it is unnecessary to remain in the chaos of turmoil, to know that Divine peace is mine in one thought, one breath, one prayer, one moment, one invitation to my Friend who is always standing by, Archangel Zoriah.

Author's note: I experienced Archangel Zoriah's energies arriving from behind, especially in my upper back, expanding up to my head, across my shoulders, down my arms, to tingling fingertips, and to the heart area. I had a strong sense of Archangel Zoriah's energies across my shoulders, almost as if Archangel Zoriah has his hands on or around my shoulders, wrapping me, or cloaking me, in the Turquoise Ray. I keenly felt the warmth and activity of the Turquoise Light in my heart area.

Chapter Eight

Indigo Ray: Success Reactivation
Archangel Uriel,
Archangel of Transformation

*Release of Self-Defeating,
Self-Destructive Behaviors.
Knowledge of Self-Worth
and Indwelling Faith.
Reconnection to the ONE.
Activation of Heartiness and Belief in Oneself.
Heartiness and Resilience.*

Opening Affirmation
*Ready and willing for superb, unlimited success, I AM.
Worthy I AM. Connected to the ONE I AM.*

Opening Prayer
I feel tired, beloved Spirit, of same old same old, and I intend more than a change—I intend a transformation for the better. Archangel Uriel, Archangel of Transformation, I invite you and the Indigo Ray for Success Reactivation into my being, in all aspects. Thank you for this transformation, from the sense of isolation and illusion of unworthiness, to this clear and open connection to Spirit and the awareness that I AM worthy and I AM holy. I intend be ever vigilant, to allow with this healing a superb unlimited ability to create and accept success, to continue to recognize myself as a Divine part of the One, to know my

worth, to be ready to move forward for my greatest joy and highest good, to manifest abundant, grand success without limit.

Invitation and Permission

I invite Archangel Uriel and the Indigo Ray for Success Reactivation into my heart, my soul, and all four bodies. I give my permission to fully allow Archangel Uriel to direct the Indigo Light to any part of all four bodies: physical, mental, spiritual and emotional, where it is most needed. I allow the Indigo Light to reawaken the DNA in my physical body.

We are never alone. We are never truly alone or isolated, though we may experience the condition of loneliness and isolation.

Beloveds, you are always in the company of Spirit, always surrounded by your angels. Whether or not you have direct consciousness of the experience, your celestial cheerleading support squad is always there (here) for you.

You **are connected** to the ONE and the ONE-NESS. Whatever else is occurring in your life, within this vital connection lies your strength, faith, courage, integrity, compassion, decency. *It is in this connection where your faith springs to life, and where your life springs to life.*

When the connection is tuned down, your decisions, actions and "slips" may begin to manifest in personal and professional ways which may not serve you well.

Let us reactivate your DNA, thereby the vital connection to the ONE. Awaken, notice and be fully present. <u>Allow success.</u>

Notice and discern your patterns of behavior and thoughts which **do serve**, and **do not serve you**. Transformation is a breath away!

Let us begin. Seek your sacred space. Begin the Holy Breath. Envision the night sky, a deep, deep dark blue indigo. The Indigo Ray is deep and radiant, flashing and glowing with its own Indigo Light, as you see stars flashing and glowing in the night sky.

Archangel Uriel, I invite you, and the Divine Indigo Ray of Success Reactivation. I call you forth to (re)awaken and transform my resting DNA of faith, hope, encouragement, and **success!**

Continue the Holy Breath. The Indigo Ray arrives as a series of lightning bolts, gentle and powerful. Feel the warmth on your upper right side.

Think of the Indigo Ray as a sort of radar or echo location—seeking and finding the dark and places which have felt neglect, and held erroneous, defeating beliefs.

The Indigo Ray seeks each of your cells and DNA strands in need of reawakening, of healing. Our Uriel, Archangel of Transformation, transforms the negative, or that which is not serving you, into the positive—into the deepest, highest levels of the One, strengthening and clearing your connection, clearing and restoring the path to success.

Continue the Holy Breath. To locate the areas which are in need of light, and to send these areas the love which they seek and long for, the Indigo Ray continues to seek and transform your cells and DNA strands, lovingly, with Divine power and authority.

Continue the Holy Breath. Like an arc of light, seeking and discovering, the Indigo Ray continues to discover, light up, reawaken, revive those areas in need of love. The cells are surrounded by arcs of light as if in an electronic circle, a radiant Indigo Ray circle of unconditional love. Awaken! Reawaken!

Continue the Holy Breath. Self-defeating and self-destructive behaviors are discovered, released as the Indigo Ray is guided by Archangel Uriel.

Continue to breathe. Worthy I AM. Holy I AM. Ready and willing I AM to move forward. Ready I AM to allow success.

Breathe the Indigo Ray in, as you would a mist. Breathe out all energies which do not serve. You do not even need to know what these energies are or where they came from.

Archangel Uriel and the Indigo Light are reawakening and transforming your connection to self and the Divine. Reigniting your awareness of your own Divine value, Archangel Uriel and the Indigo Ray also reawaken your indwelling faith—the faith you already have, which has been dormant or darkened by the *illusion* of unworthiness or disconnect.

Continue the Holy Breath. In restoring the indwelling faith, the reconnection to the One is also reactivated, cleared, restored. *Worthy I AM. Holy I AM. All the faith which I need I AM. Part of the ONE, I AM. Success I allow.*

Continue the Holy Breath. Holy I AM. Worthy I AM. *I AM worthy of unlimited success on all levels.* In reactivating your knowledge of self worth, the Indigo Ray at the same time restores your belief in yourself, re-instilling *Divine heartiness and Divine resilience.*

In the past, perhaps even when you may have been able to discern the path of success, you may have chosen a path laden with difficulty and obstacles, perhaps resulting in a "lesser" or more limited area or situation. Bless these choices and the way the choices have served you, and know that it is time to move on.

Continue the Holy Breath. Down the body, in an almost leisurely pace, the Indigo Ray moves lovingly past those bright and awakened cells, greeting and enhancing each cell with Divine love and Indigo light. The Indigo Ray is pausing now, encircling in its electric arc of light each cell, each DNA strand in need.

In this manner, the Indigo Ray can streak through some areas and amble quietly through others, pausing, encircling with radiant Indigo Light each cell and each community of cells.

Continue to breathe. Radiating through the head, throat, neck, shoulders, chest, pausing in the heart area, we continue. The Indigo Ray is energizing, moving at the perfect pace for your body, throughout your body until the tips of your toes are alive with the Indigo Light, lovingly guided by Archangel Uriel.

Feel your self tingle, especially the fingertips. Feel the electric charge in your fingertips as the Indigo Ray moves through your body. Sense yourself being raised, drawn out, drawn forward, elevated, expanded. The Indigo Ray is activating and awakening your success molecules and DNA, now liberated, now eager to move forward.

The formerly sleeping molecules and DNA cells of success are now the (re)awakened receptors, inceptors and acceptors of the Indigo Ray of Success.

Allow yourself to rest in the Indigo Ray as the Indigo Light continues its loving, holy work. Continue to breathe in the Holy Breath.

Even your heartiness and resilience are strengthened, enhanced. You are ready to move forward and manifest the success which is already yours.

Closing Affirmation
Success without limitation, I manifest.
I AM free to choose success.
Resilient, hearty, and discerning I AM.

Closing Prayer

I offer this prayer of readiness and thanks. Ready and willing I AM, without limits, to choose the bright path of success, to accept boundless success. I seek and intend to keep my connection to the ONE clear. I offer thanks for the abundance, in my mental, emotional, physical and spiritual bodies which comes from realizing that I AM part of the ONE.

Author's note: At a time of great discouragement, I felt as if I had been given a great gift, but was blocked by a sense of unworthiness in proceeding towards success. I called forth Archangel Uriel and the Indigo Ray, almost more in hope than in faith. My experience was a tremendous sense of expansion—the Indigo Ray seemed to come in through the right side of my head, and work also through my right eye. I could feel my fingertips tingle, almost the same sensation as a mild electrical charge. I also felt a flutter in my heart as the Indigo Ray continued its healing journey.

Chapter Nine

Emerald Green Ray of Purity and Infilling of Abundance
Healing the Perception of Lack

A touch of Magenta Light sparkles within the Emerald Green Ray

Archangel Raphael, Archangel of Planetary and Personal Healing

*Abundance and Purity are already yours.
You have only to manifest.*

Opening Affirmation
I AM worthy of Divine, unlimited abundance in all aspects of my life: physical, mental, emotional, spiritual, material. My clear, uncluttered connection with Spirit is my purity.

Opening Prayer
Precious Spirit, here I AM, ready for another refill of your glorious abundance. I invite Archangel Raphael, Archangel of Planetary and Personal Healing, to Divinely guide the Emerald Green Ray of Purity and Infilling of Abundance. I have so long struggled with the erroneous perception of not "having enough," not "being enough," and I call upon You for the healing of this false perception of "not enough". I place my faith and my trust in You, Precious Spirit, and in Archangel Raphael, to heal the "not enough" burden. The limitless abundance of Spirit is mine,

in all four bodies. I am delighted, grateful, and I know that I can return to the spiritual well for refills in a thought, a moment, a breath, a prayer.

Invitation and Permission
I invite Archangel Raphael and the Emerald Green Ray of Purity and Infilling of Abundance and Healing of the Perception of Lack, into my heart, my soul, and all four bodies. I give my permission to fully allow Archangel Raphael to direct the Emerald Green Light to any part of all four bodies where it is most needed. I allow the Emerald Green Light to reawaken the DNA in my physical body.

A Universe of Endlessly Abundant Miracles
A message from Tsen-Tsing

A child, looking thoughtfully into his half filled glass, was noticed by a man passing by. "Well, little boy," said the amused passer by, "Is that glass half empty or half full?" The child thought only a moment before he responded. "It doesn't matter if it's half empty or half full." The little boy beamed. "I can always go back for refills."

From Archangel Raphael: *I greet my beloveds. You are each deserving of limitless abundance. In order to manifest the abundance, we heal the perception of lack.*

The perception of lack translates into fear, which in turn translates into a greater perception of lack. Fear that we will never have *as much as we need, or* be *as much as we need, or* not receive and enjoy *the abundance we desire. The fear increases. Break this cycle, beloveds.*

What are purity and abundance? Purity is the perfect alignment of your God-self, your Christed self, with Spirit. Purity is the abundance of clarity in the connection with God.

Abundance is the awareness and energy of having all that you need, in every breath, in every thought, in every manifestation of your mental, spiritual, emotional and physical bodies.

Spirit pours limitless refills of abundance into each of our bodies, souls, lives. Let us be as open as we can, to receive as much as we can.

The Emerald Light possesses the key to unlock and reactivate the DNA within our body and our soul for a deeper healing, to open and clear our connection to the One, allowing purity and abundance.

Out loud, beloveds. Let's heal it all. I AM worthy to receive and enjoy Divine abundance. Limitless abundance, I AM. Purity I AM.

In your sacred space, get comfortable. Begin the Holy Breath. *I invite Archangel Raphael and the Emerald Green Ray for Purity and Infilling of Abundance, and Healing for the Perception of Lack, in this moment.*

I invite Archangel Raphael and the Emerald Green Ray to unlock and (re)activate my DNA for a deeper healing in all four bodies.

Continue the Holy Breath. We must first heal the perception of lack. Following the healing of the perception of lack, we re-pour, refill, without limit, the knowledge of abundance in all four bodies.

The energies of the Emerald Green Light arrive in the lower head and upper back area. Archangel Raphael is directing the light to expand, and diffuse into each part of the body. You are, in fact, already radiant with Green Light.

Continue the Holy Breath. Feel the heat at the back of your head. Feel the Emerald Green Ray expanding, filling your head with light.

Continue the Holy Breath. The shimmering Emerald Ray is expanding down the neck, the shoulders, into your heart area. Continue to breathe. The Emerald Light continues, now, expanding down your body, down to your legs, down to the soles of your feet.

Breathe. Your entire being is infused with loving Light. As the Emerald Light radiates within you, the healing for the perception of lack begins.

In the physical, mental, emotional and spiritual bodies, the infilling of limitless Divine abundance is present. With your every breath, DNA is unlocked. Emerald Green Light pours forth Divine abundance, Divine connection.

Continue the Holy Breath. Let us begin the healing of the perception of lack in the **mental body**. We heal, in this moment, the perception of lack of soundness of mind. The Emerald Light infuses every aspect of the mental body with the healing light, with the Divine reminder, the Divine reawaken-er.

Your cells and DNA are revitalized, reawakened *to the clear connection, to the abundance of Spirit.* Continue to breathe. *Holy I AM. Valuable and worthy I AM. I have all that I need in any moment.* Divine healing with the Emerald light, in each cell, each DNA strand, is taking place with your every breath.

Continue to breathe. Archangel Raphael and the shimmering Emerald Green Ray are infilling the abundance of self-worth, the awareness of the infinite abundance, and abundance of soundness of mind.

Continue the Holy Breath. In the *emotional body*, Archangel Raphael heals the perception of weakness, "not being good enough." Breathe in the Light. Now breathe in the infilling of abundance of strength and clarity.

Strength and clarity heal and replace, with Spirit's unconditional love, the sense of isolation, of not being enough, of separation. *I AM a radiant spark of Spirit. I AM connected to the*

ONE, perfectly and clearly. The ONE is perfectly, clearly connected to me.

Breathe in the Emerald Green Light as it discovers, loves, and revives each cell living in the illusion of aloneness. *I Am worthy of love, I AM Divine unconditional love without beginning, without end. I AM beloved. I Am part of the ONE.*

Continue to breathe. Archangel Raphael and the Emerald Green Ray restore, refill, *infill* your spirit and emotional body with an abundance of clarity, a powerful, open connection, and strength. *I AM an abundance of clarity. I AM strong.*

Continue to breathe. In the **physical body**, the perception of lack of energy, of vitality, of well being is healed. The Emerald Green Ray is seeking the cells and DNA strands which have given up, believing themselves to be overcome, exhausted, disconnected, insufficient.

Continue the Holy Breath. Archangel Raphael and the Emerald Green Ray infuse each cell and DNA strand with the vivid Emerald Light, with the truth: I AM abundant vitality. I AM abundant, radiant health. I rejoice in an abundance of general well being.

Continue the Holy Breath. In the **spiritual body**, the perception of lack of connection is healed.

The Emerald Green Ray, sparkling with magenta tones, seeks the wounds in the spiritual body, where the belief in disconnect and disheartenment have created the illusion of a muddied or broken connection to Spirit. The Emerald Light again seeks, finds, and rejuvenates each aspect of the spiritual body which is disheartened.

A great infilling of an abundance of clarity and awareness occurs: *I AM part of the ONE. I AM connected to the ONE.*

Herein lies the purity: the clarity of the connection to the ONE! Your connection is revitalized, restored!

Continue the Holy Breath. Abundance is having all that you need at the time you need it. *Abundance is also your*

awareness of your ability to readily return to the well for another refill of even more abundance.
Abundant I AM. Abundant WE ARE in any moment; ready for a refill with a thought, a prayer, and invitation, and a breath. Archangel Raphael is waiting, delighting in your next invitation.

Closing Affirmation
I AM a vital recipient of Divine abundance in a Universe of endlessly abundant miracles. I have all that I need and more, in any moment, in all aspects of my life. I AM far more than enough. I have far more than enough.

Closing Prayer
Thank you, Spirit and Archangel Raphael, for the deep healing in all four of my bodies, and for the limitless abundance in my life. I intend to return often, whenever needed, to Archangel Raphael, to re-access, reclaim, the limitless abundance of the Universe, which is already my gift from Spirit, in all four of my bodies. I intend and I pray that I will, daily, with thought and action, turn to Spirit, refreshing my purity, my connection, understanding even more fully the understanding of limitless abundance in all parts of my life.

Author's note: I experienced the Emerald Green Ray to be warm and subtle. As with Archangel Raphael's Jade Green Ray, I felt the energies arrive in my upper back area, and the warmth spread, or expand, to my chest, my heart area, my shoulders and arms. I could feel my heart beating, and my fingertips tingle with the energies.

Chapter Ten

Jade Green Ray
Healing Of Internal and External (Physical) Injuries

Archangel Raphael, Archangel of Planetary and Personal Healing

Suffering is unnecessary.

Opening Affirmation
Unconditional Divine Love I AM.
Unconditionally healed I AM.
Divinely focused, I AM.

Opening Prayer
Archangel Raphael, Archangel of Planetary and Personal Healing, I invite you to Divinely present and guide the Jade Green Ray in this moment. Into the radiant Jade Green Light and the energies of Archangel Raphael I offer my sincerity, my authenticity, my prayer for healing at this time. I present my perfect clarity of intention to receive and rejoice in the Divine healing. I request to be surprised by unexpected further Divine healings and miracles. I offer my thanks.

Invitation and Permission
I invite Archangel Raphael and the Jade Green Ray for the Healing of Internal and External Physical Injuries into my heart, my soul, and all four bodies. I give my permission to fully allow Archangel Raphael to direct the Jade Green Light to any part of

all four bodies where it is most needed. I allow the Jade Green Light to reawaken the DNA in my physical body.

From Archangel Raphael: *Beloveds, we are in a state of Divine love, empathy and compassion for you at all times. In your time of wound and injury, we especially await your invitation for a healing.*
Divine healing is yours for the asking. All you need is a minute particle of faith, a minute particle of trust, and an invitation. Let's get going!

Many of your physicians are blessed and work in concert with Spirit. Always consult a physician if you sense the need.

Call forth both the physician's angels and your angels to inspire your physician to discern and act upon the best course of action, and to take the time needed to serve you best.

Appropriate medications, treatments, meditations and healing rays work together. You do not diminish, but rather enhance, each, by blessing their work in exquisite harmony.

Seek your sacred space. Begin the Holy Breath. In through the nose. Out through the mouth. Breathe in God. Breathe out all energies not serving you.

Call forth Archangel Raphael, Archangel of Planetary and Personal Healing. Archangel Raphael, I call you forth in this moment, with the Jade Green Ray for the Healing of Internal an External Physical Injuries. Envision the soft, vibrant color of the Jade Green stone.

Continue the Holy Breath. Feel the Jade Green Ray for your healing come in through the back of your head. Feel an expansion, warmth, your fingertips tingle. Notice the general sense of being uplifted, physically and spiritually.

Continue the Holy Breath. Hold the particular area, for which you seek healing, in your awareness. Allow the Jade Green Ray, with the guidance of Archangel Raphael, to first make a clean sweep—a physiological survey—of the body, a Divine body

Jade Green Ray

scan. *I give Archangel Raphael my permission for the Divine body scan.*

Archangel Raphael is guiding the Jade Green Ray down the body, pausing, investigating, diagnosing each cell, each muscle, nerve, each part of your body.

Continue the Holy Breath. Archangel Raphael continues the diagnostic journey—what has been injured or wounded? What may be in a condition of dis-ease? What is in need of Divine healing?

Continue the Holy Breath. Feel the ray as it moves slowly down your body, expanding, radiating health and vitality, all the way down to the tips of your toes.

Rest. Allow Archangel Raphael to do the Holy work of healing, in those areas of which you are aware, and not aware.

Continue the Holy Breath. Focus the ray to the particular area which is injured, and giving you discomfort. Dis-ease, or feeling unwell, can also be considered a form of physical injury. Archangel Raphael treats and heals it all.

Let us make an example: you lifted something, and a back injury has occurred. Focus on the area of discomfort. *Archangel Raphael, my back hurts.*

As Archangel Raphael is guiding the Jade Green Ray to the area of injury, focus your love and appreciation on the injured area. Thank the injured area, in this case the back, for all of the times it has served you, done its best for you, even when you have not paid attention or appreciated the injured area.

Archangel Raphael is bathing, soothing, restoring the injured area with the luminescent light, with the Divine energies, of the Jade Green Ray.

Continue the Holy Breath. The Jade Green Ray seeks and enfolds in its radiant light each molecule, each cell. Continue to send your own unconditional love to the injured area, thanking the injured area and expressing appreciation once again for all the service it has given you.

Archangel Raphael continues the healing of the injured area with the Jade Green Ray, until the healing is complete.

You may be complete in this moment, or it is possible that Archangel Raphael my have diagnosed another injury, internal or external. Ask Archangel Raphael: are there further injuries which need healing in this moment?

Breathe. Archangel Raphael will let you know if the healing is complete, or if healing needs to be continued.

If you are complete with the Jade Green Ray, offer your thanks to Archangel Raphael and the Jade Green Ray. Continue to send love, appreciation and light to the healed area.

If Archangel Raphael has diagnosed another injury, continue the Holy Breath. Archangel Raphael asks your permission to heal any other injuries discovered during the Divine diagnostic tour of the body.

Continue to breathe in the Jade Green Ray. *Archangel Raphael, I invite you, with the healing energies of the Jade Green Ray, to continue to heal any other injuries you have discovered in this moment.*

Continue the Holy Breath. The Jade Green Ray continues, with the loving, nurturing guidance of Archangel Raphael, to soothe, to relieve, to heal other injuries in the body.

Continue to breathe and notice where the Jade Green Ray is resting, healing. If you are not noticing the particular area, simply accept the healing, and thank your entire body for its service to you. Once again, offer your thanks to the injured area, wherever it may be, and to your entire body for its service to you.

As your body serves you, serve your body with kindness and love. Thank Archangel Raphael for Divine healings and miracles. Thank Spirit for the abundance of radiant good health.

Closing Affirmation

*Miracles of Divine healing are manifest in my life, strengthened with each conscious breath. With the radiance of the healing Jade Green Ray,
I AM healed.*

Closing Prayer

I accept and I AM grateful for Divine healings manifest in this moment, and those which are miraculously arriving as the energies of my Divine encounter with Archangel Raphael and the Jade Green Ray continue to integrate. I decree each breath a conscious connection to the Divine, deepening my healing, my strength, my acceptance of the healing, and my faith.

Author's note: The Jade Green Ray, for me, arrived in a mode of expansion. I could feel it at the lower part of the back of my head. Instead of feeling it move through my body, as sometimes is the experience with other rays, I felt a true sense of expansion—simply expanding across my head, chest, the rest of my body, and I felt the warmth in injured area for which I requested the healing.

    I found the Jade Green color almost too subtle to envision. It may be an idea to stop by a store and look at a piece of Jade Green jewelry or a jade green stone to get a clearer image of the Jade Green Ray.

Chapter Eleven

The Golden Ray, The Christed Light
*Enlightenment, Compassion, Illumination,
Unconditional Love
Joyfulness and Gratitude in Every Breath*
Holy Friend Jesus, and Cosmic Buddha

*A reminder also of your Divine value and your
Divine ONE-NESS.
Jesus wants you to know:
I am your devoted Friend Jesus,
not your "Master" Jesus.*

Opening Affirmation
I enjoy the enlightenment, compassion, illumination and unconditional love of the ONE. I AM perfect in God. I AM a perfect part of the ONE.

Opening Prayer
I invite Holy Friend Jesus and Holy Friend Cosmic Buddha to reignite and reaffirm within me my awareness and knowledge of my place in the Universe, as a precious part of the ONE, with the Golden Ray, the Christed Light. With every step, help me to continue to recognize my own Divinity and my own worth, and to express my Divinity through genuine Divine compassion and Divine unconditional love. Sharing the good company of Jesus and Cosmic Buddha, I intend to experience and express joyfulness and connection to the ONE, illumination and gratitude in every breath.

Invitation and Permission

I invite Holy Friend Jesus, Cosmic Buddha, and the Golden Ray of Enlightenment, Compassion, Illumination, Unconditional Love, Joyfulness and Gratitude in every breath into my heart, my soul, and all four bodies. I give my permission to fully allow Holy Friend Jesus and the Cosmic Buddha to direct the Golden Light to any part of all four bodies where it is most needed. I allow the Golden Light to reawaken the DNA in my physical body.

Together, Cosmic Buddha and Friend Jesus arrive with an important message for you: *We come with our Golden Ray,* **not to suddenly instill within you perfection in Spirit; rather to remind you that you are already perfect in God.** *You are perfect in Spirit. As a child of God, how can you be less than worthy?*

We reawaken, even to the very DNA fibers, the consciousness within your mind, body, soul and heart that you are, in fact, already the physical embodiment of Divine unconditional love; already part of the ONE, already Divinely beloved!

Out loud, beloveds, affirm: *I AM Perfect in God. Perfect I AM. I AM Divinely beloved. Divinely beloved, I AM. I AM Holy. Holy I AM. I AM Worthy. Worthy I AM.*

You, Cosmic Buddha and Jesus, are each part of each other and part of the One. Jesus and Cosmic Buddha, represent, embody, and are both an equally vital part of the Golden Ray.

Seek and enjoy your sacred place. You deserve this time with Spirit. Begin the Holy Breath.

Holy Friend Jesus and Cosmic Buddha, I invite you with your Golden Ray, your Christed Light. The two best Friends delight in your invitation.

Jesus and Cosmic Buddha both want you to know: *Our separation from one another is an illusion. Envision us walking*

The Golden Ray, The Christed Light

towards you, arm in arm, smiling. Your separation from us is also an illusion: **we are all great Friends, all a part of each other.** *A heavenly, cosmic trio.*
Continue the Holy Breath. Radiantly Golden Light, Golden Glow, Golden smiles approach you as Jesus and Cosmic Buddha continue to walk closer to you, arm in arm. *Jesus and Cosmic Buddha are here to serve you, to reignite and reaffirm for you who you are in the Universe—***you are part of the ONE**.
Continue to breathe. Jesus is on your right; Cosmic Buddha is on your left. Together, the three of you create a vibrant, Divine Circle. The Golden Light of the two Friends illuminates you and radiates around and within you. You glow as well.
Continue the Holy Breath. Place your hands comfortably at your sides, palms up, ready to hold hands with your Friends.
The Golden energies lovingly embrace you. Continue to breathe, to envision your central location in the Divine Circle. Jesus is on your right, placing His hand in your open hand. Cosmic Buddha is on your left, is placing His hand in your open hand. Holy Friend Jesus and the Cosmic Buddha, in turn have joined hands, their two energies, and yours, now form a perfect circle, a Divine ONE.
You are truly in the center of an ultimate Divine Circle, symbolically and in fact, being held, loved and supported beyond measure by two of your Divine Friends.
Affirm and remind yourself: I AM Holy. Holy I AM. I AM Worthy. Worthy I AM. I AM Perfect in God. Perfect I AM. A vibrant part of the One, I AM. Truly blessed with my own Divine energies, and the Divine energies of Friend Jesus and Cosmic Buddha, I AM.
Our Golden Ray surrounds you, within and without, and enfolds you. **We reawaken and resurrect, within your heart, your mind and in your soul, and reactivate the very DNA of your being.** *To your truth and awareness: you are already*

worthy, unconditionally Divinely beloved, a Divine Golden part of the Divine ONE.

We ask you once more, beloveds: How could you be less than worthy? You are not only a child of God, you are in fact a spark of God—a part of the great ONE of which we are each a part, including myself, Jesus, who is speaking to your heart and soul at this moment.

We tell you in this moment, and in all moments, you are each a perfect child of God. I AM Holy. Holy I AM. I AM Worthy. Worthy I AM. I AM Perfect in God. Perfect I AM. Part of the ONE, I AM. Blessed, I AM.

Know yourself to be surrounded, illuminated, in a stunning Golden glow, with Jesus energetically holding you, holding your hand, on the right side, and Cosmic Buddha, energetically holding you, holding your hand, on your left. Enjoy yourself as you continue to be the center of the Divine Circle, of the ONE.

Continue the Holy Breath. The Golden energies enter from the top of your head, radiating, reigniting, reaffirming your connection, a part of the ONE in the Universe, reminding each cell, each DNA fiber of who you truly are.

Continue the Holy Breath as the Golden Ray moves. *Our Golden Ray encompasses unconditional love for self as well as for others.* The Golden Ray moves down the brain, the eyes, the ears, the mouth, the throat.

Our Golden Ray offers illumination, awakens Divine compassion, within Divine, unconditional love. Compassion for self and others and all living beings, including the planet. Our Golden Ray reawakens gratitude, to be fully presenting each moment of your life. Notice and enjoy everything!

What is compassion? The caring for another as we must care for ourselves, Divinely loving ourselves and others, expressing Divine love.

What is gratitude? The recognition of all that is holy around us and the gladness in our hearts.

Golden Ray illuminates, reawakens and reminds your heart, your soul, each cell, and every fiber of DNA in your being of your own Divine unconditional love, compassion for self and all living beings. Continue to breathe.

Illuminating, shining, brightening, and radiating, the Golden Ray continues to move through the head, the throat, to the heart. Don't rush the energies—rest, relax, allowing the Golden Ray to move and rest as guided by our two Holy Friends.

Continue the Holy Breath. The Golden Ray continues to radiate, to glow, through the solar plexus, down, though the legs, even to the tips of your toes.

You are still and always in the perfect Circle of Divine Light.

The Golden Ray offered by Holy Friend Jesus and Cosmic Buddha, is for Divine unconditional love and compassion and healing of self, of others, of conditions such as war, and healing on a global level.

Your feet know the Golden glow and have knowledge of the Golden path; your hands, you arms, with Golden energies radiating, have all that is Divine within reach—nothing exceeds the grasp of your Divine Golden hands.

The refreshment of the Golden Ray is yours in any moment. Simply invite your Friends Jesus and Cosmic Buddha.

Your life is your own. I AM always with you to light the path—the choice to continue to step upon the Golden path is yours.

Closing Affirmation

I AM a radiant part of the Divine Circle, of the ONE. Perfect in Spirit, I (already) AM. My truth, as a vital part of the ONE, I AM.

Closing Prayer

I pray the prayer of acceptance and thanks. I accept that I AM an integral part of Spirit, that I AM an integral and important part of the ONE. I intend to use the Golden Light to continue to discern the Golden Path. Help me <u>to be willing to be willing,</u> to live my Divine truth out loud in actions, thoughts and deeds, as a living embodiment of Spirit and the ONE. I form my hands in a circle, my expression and reminder that I AM a vibrant part of the ONE with smiling and delighted Friend Jesus on my right, Cosmic Buddha on my left. I AM in the middle of the Divine circle, a Divine expression of Golden energies, serving the Light, myself and others.

Author's note: The energies entered very gently from the top of my head, warming the right side. I could feel a physical sense of expansion as my head and the energies moved out through the arms, to the tips of my fingers.

The Golden glow continued to move down, resting for a while in my solar plexus.

I experienced the image of holding Jesus' hand, with my own hand, and Cosmic Buddha's hand with my other—physical, tingling sensation. I could mostly feel the Golden glow in the chest, heart, solar plexus, and in my head—a true sense of expansion. I found this healing ray both intense and gentle.

Chapter Twelve

Silver Ray: Healing, Purity, Abundance and Joy
Anarashia, The Silver One, Goddess of Peace, Justice and Mercy
As Jesus is to the Gold, Anarashia is to the Silver

*Rejoice and rest in the celestial hammock of Silver Ray strands,
woven for you by Anarashia, the Silver One.*

Opening Affirmation
*Purity I AM. Peace I AM.
Unlimited abundance and joy, I AM.
Healed and Healer, I AM.*

Opening Prayer
Anarashia, Silver One, Goddess of Peace, Justice and Mercy, I invite you and the Silver Ray of Healing, Purity, Abundance and Joy into my being, reawakening my very DNA, to create this healing. Beloved Spirit, restore within me the peaceful flowing stream replacing the tumultuous raging waters which sometimes seemingly carry my emotions, feelings and thoughts away. In the cacophony of sounds, voices, demands and discord, help me to

discern clearly the harmony of Your voice, the quiet, melodic voices of the Holy Masters and Angels, Comfort me with Your peace, Your healing. Restore my joy, my awareness and intention of abundance, as I rest upon Silver Ray strands, woven for me by Anarashia, Goddess of Peace, Justice and Mercy. Within the Silver rest, restore my energies into purity, so that I may know peace, abundance and joy.

Invitation and Permission

I invite Anarashia, the Silver One, and the Silver Ray of Healing, Purity, Abundance and Joy into my heart, my soul, and all four bodies. I give my permission to fully allow Anarashia to direct the Silver Light to any part of all four bodies where it is most needed. I allow the Silver Light to reawaken the DNA in my physical body.

Beloveds! Welcome to this healing, to the lovingly fierce focus of the Silver Ray and the Goddess Anarashia. Anarashia is to the Silver as Jesus is to the Gold.

Healing, purity, abundance and joy are integrated energies, as are many from Spirit.

When you offer or receive a healing, energy, purity, abundance and joy are also offered or received. Never traveling alone, Divine energies of healing, abundance, joy and purity keep each other Divine company. Invite one, and the other three arrive as welcome guests.

Beloveds, what do we mean by purity and abundance? Purity is complete rest in Spirit, clarity and open connection to Spirit, knowledge of Spirit, with no encumbrances and debris creating static.

Peace occurs with the restoration of purity. Abundance is a vital aspect of peace and purity.

Joy is your gift from the Divine, reawakened, revitalized by Anarashia and Her Silver Ray.

Peace and purity allow you to tap into (recognize your One-ness) the great abundance of Spirit. How much abundance does Spirit have available to you, in this or any moment? Limitless, without beginning, without end, immeasurable, infinite, in all four bodies, in all aspects of your life.

Each of you, beloveds, is a healer of self and others, with a burning desire to heal and be healed, even in this moment. You have only to manifest your gifts.

Let us begin the meditation for Healing, Purity, Abundance and Joy. Seek your sacred space. Relax, be comfortable. We are in for a spectacular ride together with Spirit, with Anarashia, the Silver One.

Begin the Holy Breath. *Anarashia, Silver One, Goddess of Peace, Justice and Mercy, I invite You, with your Silver Ray of Healing, Purity, Abundance and Joy, to reawaken and transform my entire being in all four bodies, reawakening my very DNA, to experience healing, purity, abundance and joy in every aspect of my being.*

Continue to breathe. Envision a brilliant Silver Laser Light. The Silver Ray, laser sharp in focus, and power tool strong, enters through the heart, enveloping the heart in Silver healing radiant energy.

Continue the Holy Breath. Feel the Silver Ray, as you breathe, radiate out to your hands. Continue to breathe. The energies of Anarashia and the Silver Ray are radiating from the palms of your hands. You can feel the healing heat of the Silver Ray radiating.

Healing of self is essential. Let's begin, then, with the healing of self, and next move on to the healing of others.

Continue the Holy Breath. Feel the Silver Stream of Light continue to pulsate in the palms of your hands.

Focus, concentrate on the Silver Ray energies of Purity, Healing, Joy and Abundance—the Divine traveling companions, *outflowing* from you palms, fingers, even from your fingertips.

Allow the Silver Ray to radiate through your hands. Place your hands slowly over your head, sharply focusing the four energies of healing, joy, purity and abundance over your head. Everything inside your head beloveds, every cell, every DNA strand, is receiving these powerful laser energies.

Continue to breathe. Move your hands now, over your ears, your face, your eyes, and over your throat, pausing, radiating the four Divine energies of healing, joy, abundance and purity. Pause where the Goddess Anarashia guides you to pause.

Continue the Holy Breath. Place your hands, as they move down, over your heart. Your heart, beloved, has been waiting, longing to receive Anarashia's Silver Ray and the Silver energies of joy, purity, abundance and healing. Continue the Holy Breath as you hold your hands over your heart.

Goddess Anarashia has another gift for you now. Anarashia has created a celestial hammock, woven of Silver strands for you. Envision yourself completely at rest in these moments, enveloped in Anarashia's Silver hammock and her loving energies of healing, purity, abundance and joy.

Continue to breathe. The Silver Ray continues to light up your heart, a Silvery Flood Light, shining and lighting up those heart spaces darkened by anger, resentment, doubt, and worry.

Continue to place your hands over your heart. Radiating, the Silver Light from your hands continues to heal with the energies of abundance, joy, purity and healing.

You are enfolded in the Silver Ray, in the celestial hammock of shining Silver strands. Supported, relaxed and at peace in Anarashia's resting place, you receive and manifest Divine healings.

Continue to breathe. Not by acts of will or determination can a healing be compelled. Only by sweet surrender do you *allow* Anarashia's Silver Ray to continue to radiate within you and do its healing work.

Continue the Holy Breath; continue to rest in your Silver hammock. As you rest, feel yourself continue to be infused with the Silver Light. Rest, delight and have fun in the Silver hammock. When you feel complete, we can turn our attention to the healing of others.

A note, beloveds. **Before healing others, take the time you need to first heal yourself, in mental, emotional, spiritual and physical bodies, with the Silver Ray energies.**

Continue the Holy Breath. Goddess Anarashia and the Silver Ray energies are still with you.

As you continue to breathe in the Silver Ray of Healing, Purity, Abundance and Joy, the energies radiate from your heart into your hands. Turn your hands outwards, towards the person you wish to heal, or the situation you wish to bless or heal.

Continue the Holy Breath. As a healer, focus and concentrate on the Silver Ray energies of Healing, Purity, Abundance and Joy radiating from your hands.

Continue the Holy Breath. Focus on the recipient—on the person or situation you wish to heal.

Continue the Holy Breath. Envision intensely focused laser beams of Silver Light, and send the Silver Ray to the recipient, with the unconditional Divine love of a healer, guided by the fierce focus of Anarashia.

As the healer of self and healer of others, you are Divine.

Closing Affirmation
Abundance without limit, I AM.
Joyful, uplifted, and filled with peace and purity, I AM.
Healer and healed, I AM.

Closing Prayer
I accept and I AM grateful for the peace, abundance, purity and joy brought to me by Anarashia and the Silver Ray. I intend to return to the Silver One, in any moment, with a breath and an invitation. I know the celestial Silver Ray hammock, woven for me

by Anarashia, Goddess of Peace, Justice and Mercy, is ready and waiting to recharge the energies of this Silver Ray healing. Strengthen me in every breath with the Silver Ray energies of peace, purity, abundance and joy, to be a Divine expression of these precious Silver Ray healing energies, in everything I do and to everyone I meet. I pray that I AM a Divine instrument not only to further manifest, but to perceive the Divine energies of peace, abundance, joy and purity to all beings, to all life, on this planet.

Author's note: Wow. In my experience, while other healing rays are sometimes subtle, Goddess Anarashia and the Silver Ray arrive in a very strong fashion, for me, in my heart, causing a few butterflies. I could quickly feel the pulsating in the palms of my hands as the Silver Ray radiated, and I could also feel the heat emanating from my hands and fingers when I brought them near my head, face and heart.

Chapter Thirteen

Orange Ray of Creativity
Creativity in all aspects, at all times.
Archangel Jophiel,
Archangel of Illumination

Joy is a part of creativity. Have some fun, for heaven's sake!
Limitation is an illusion of the past.
Step lightly with your own holy power—your own
I AM.

Opening Affirmation
Fun I AM. Living my joy I AM. Creativity without limit I AM. I AM open to receive, in each breath, every creative dimension of thought, prayer, inspiration, perspective. Creativity radiates from my heart, soul, spirit and mind. New aspects I AM. New aspects I notice. Radiant awareness without limit I AM.

Opening Prayer
Spirit, here I AM, standing worthy and holy, before you: open hearted, open minded, open spirited, to receive the multitude of creative gifts which you offer. Archangel Jophiel, I invite you and the Orange Ray of Creativity into my very soul, to resurrect creativity within me, in all aspects of my being. Help me to be daring enough to notice and act upon the creativity (re)awakened within myself and others, to be aware of solutions, opportunities

and new facets presented to me. *As many facets of a jewel shimmer, so Your gifts shimmer before me also. I thank You.*

Invitation and Permission
I invite Archangel Jophiel and the Orange Ray of Creativity into my heart, my soul, and all four bodies. I give my permission to fully allow Archangel Jophiel to direct the Orange Light to any part of all four bodies where it is most needed. I allow the Orange Light to reawaken the DNA in my physical body.

Creativity is Divine energy. Divine energy is fun, and this world needs more fun! We do not always need to set goals or define a certain outcome. Be creative just for the fun of it. All else will follow. **FUN I AM!** **Have some fun, for heaven's sake! Enjoy your joy!**

Let's have some fun. Lighten Up! *Break free of stuck.* Let us not view this adventure into creativity as serious. Seek new aspects of change, change, change.

Break out of the stuck, into the *lightning force of forward movement*, with breathtaking speed.

Creativity is not only "for artists," or only about art, sculpture, design, or writing. Creativity is about approaching, with verve and vitality, each aspect of our lives, inner and outer, with a fresh eye. Examine each aspect, attack and change, *transform*.

Take a good look, and see what you did not see before. A new perspective empowers you to act upon a course which you had not previously envisioned.

Perhaps you desire a change, and can not find the path. Archangel Jophiel and the Orange Ray of Creativity are ready to serve you. We start first on the personal level. If you choose, you can then move to the community and global levels.

As an example, consider your relationship with your children, spouse, lover, friend, job, the way you perceive yourself to look, or to be in the world. Consider the aspect(s) in which you feel stuck in the muck.

Where do you feel engulfed or immobilized? Choose from any one of an infinite number of areas in which you desire a change. At this moment, let us use relationships as an example.

Seek your sacred space. Begin the Holy Breath. If you are out and about, create a sacred space with the Holy Breath, and invite Archangel Jophiel and the Orange Ray wherever you are, in any moment of need.

Archangel Jophiel, I call you forth. I call forth the Orange Ray of Creativity.

Breathe in the Orange Ray. Allow the Orange Ray to fill every molecule, every particle of your being. Archangel Jophiel is with you now, and glad of your company.

Continue the Holy Breath. Feel the Orange Ray moving through you with purpose, with method, with joy. *Joy is a part of creativity.*

Now focus the Orange Ray in your brain. You are not compelling or demanding. You are *allowing* your brain to think about the relationship differently than before.

View the relationship as you would view a precious gem. What new angles, what new aspects, shimmer before you, previously unseen?

The same relationship looks different now. Focus on the shimmering aspect. In what new light do you view, perceive this new aspect or perspective? The shimmering aspect can even reveal new perspective, which offers you thought and direction for a new course of action.

Allow the Orange Ray to continue to rest in your brain. Continue to breathe. Envision the vibrant Orange Ray, and its warmth, radiating to your eyes. You now see the relationship more clearly, *without judgment, but with discernment.*

Orange Ray, rest in my ears. Place a filter of creativity in my ears. I *listen* more clearly with compassion, creativity, depth and discernment to that which I hear.

Orange Ray, rest in my throat. I have something different to speak, and in a different tone of voice (perhaps more understanding and less judgmental) than before.

Orange Ray, radiate into to my heart. Rest and illumine there.

Allow Archangel Jophiel and the Orange Ray of Creativity to radiate in your heart, to joyfully outshine fear, doubt, negativity and cynicism. The Orange Ray loosens and disengages the sense of rigid stuck.

How does the Orange Ray of Creativity affect the heart? Archangel Jophiel: *We wrap the heart in Divine Light. We penetrate each cell, each molecule, and each DNA strand with Divine illumination, with the Orange Ray of Creativity.*

Wrapped in Divine Light and Illumination, and with the Orange Ray radiating, rest. You do not need to will, try, force, or compel. Simply rest. Allow your newly discovered creativity *to be*. Archangel Jophiel safely holds your heart now, illuminating and radiating love and joy.

The Orange Ray opens the heart, seeks the truth, and reveals the truth of the situation upon which you are focused. Once clearly seen through the energies of light, the resolution of the situation and the creative course of action needed for change will become apparent.

It is here, within the Orange Ray in your heart and in your mind that you will be amazed as your creative abilities are revealed. The course of action will snap into focus.

How does the Orange Ray clear away cloudy resistance? Archangel Jophiel loves resistance, and asks you to join with His angelic powers and energies. *Together, love the resistance.* The resistance, through light and love, is *transformed* into your willingness to act.

The Divine Light and the Orange Ray energies clear the resistance, flummox, perceived barriers, at your invitation, with your authenticity. Open yourself, your heart, your mind, your body, to the Orange Ray, to creative solution, presented through truth and love.

Thank Spirit for the Orange Ray. As you release the clouds of resistance, know that the glow of Archangel Jophiel's Orange Ray remains with you.

The shimmering creative aspect is revealed. Not through judgment, not through will. Through love. The creative course is always the course lovingly navigated, lovingly mapped out.

Pay attention to creative thoughts, ideas and solutions as they are presented to you, perhaps in unusual ways, perhaps through comments, insights, music. Have fun noticing!

Creativity is a gift to be enjoyed and employed, constantly and consistently. You are a walking rainbow, a streaming fountain of creative ideas in each aspect of your life. Limitation is an illusion of the past.

Call on Archangel Jophiel and the Orange Ray at any time, at any moment.

Allow the Orange Ray to reveal the creative solution. Allow yourself to be delighted, surprised, and to trust in the creative path set before you.

Consider inviting the Orange Ray and Archangel Jophiel for creativity in global solutions as well as personal.

Know that your navigators are holy, and love you in every moment. *Creative I AM. Holy I AM. Worthy I AM.*

Archangel Jophiel asks you to *remember to step lightly, with your own holy power, your own I AM. Remember also:* **FUN I AM! *Have some fun, for heaven's sake!***

Closing Affirmation
FUN I AM. Infinitely creative, I AM.
Exquisitely aware and alert to creative inspirations, I AM.

Closing Prayer
I AM grateful to restore more FUN and creativity in each aspect of my life. Spirit, I intend to be aware, at each turn, in each moment, of the creative solutions, ideas, and miracles which You send my way. I clearly intend to invite and allow Divine inspiration and Divine creativity in all aspects, in all moments of my life. I thank the Divine and Archangel Jophiel for the miracles and gifts manifested. I choose to enjoy these gifts, not only to serve myself, but to serve others as well.

Author's note: I experienced the Orange Ray of Creativity as very warm and vibrant, arriving through the right side of my upper body. The warmth of the Orange Ray seemed to expand throughout my back, to my heart area, down my shoulders to my fingertips. I also experienced the energies of Archangel Jophiel and the Orange Ray as moving down my chest to my solar plexus, all the way down to my lower body. I had a physical sensation of the presence of the Orange Ray and Archangel Jophiel all around me.

Chapter Fourteen

Auburn Ray: To Instill and Awaken Organizational Skills and Abilities

Clearing, Cleansing and Reorganization of Inner and Outer Clutter
Archangel Zoriel, Messenger of God

Order In, Clutter Out. Let's Get It Together.
Distill stuff to instill liberation.

Archangel Zoriel asks you to consider whether it is better to run on light, winged feet; or to trudge, heavily burdened, through the mud.

Disorganization is a form of imprisonment.
Organization is a form of freedom and peace.

Opening Affirmation
I have more than I need. I AM free from imprisonment of things and "stuff." My inner vision is clear and radiant. I AM liberated.

Opening Prayer
I AM grateful and bless all that I have. I intend to have freedom in all aspects of my life. Please reveal to me my liberation from "stuff". Help me to bless and release attachment to those things which no longer serve me, and which may serve others. Place into my awareness the perfect arrangements of time and energy, to create more of each, to enjoy myself and have more FUN.

Show me how I can do more with less effort, and leave more time for joy and fun in all aspects my life. Sweep away my inner clutter; liberate me from ideas and commitments which do not serve me, so I can see clearly the path ahead, that I may serve myself and others. Archangel Zoriel, Messenger of God, I invite you and the Auburn Ray into my heart and into my soul in this sacred time of healing.

Invitation and Permission
I invite Archangel Zoriel and the Auburn Ray to Instill and Awaken Organizational Skills and Abilities into my heart, my soul, and all four bodies. I give my permission to fully allow Archangel Zoriel to direct the Auburn Light to any part of all four bodies where it is most needed. I allow the Auburn Light to reawaken the DNA in my physical body.

Beloveds: as a person, gasping, drowns at sea, many of us are drowning in "stuff" and disorganization in our environment, energies, time and efforts.

We do not ask you to conduct your lives in a manner of absolute precision and inflexibility, without the joy of spontaneity. *We desire for you to be in command of your freedom in every moment, as you are free in Spirit.*

Rather, we ask you be fully present, and notice in your life: where are you slowed down? Where are you frustrated?

Look around in this moment. Are you feeling good about what you see, what you *need* to do, what you *want* to do; or do you feel overwhelmed, disheartened and stuck? Lighten up! Get yourselves together!

Disorganization is a form of imprisonment. Organization is a form of freedom and peace.

We begin by calling forth Archangel Zoriel and the Auburn Ray. Seek your sacred space.

Auburn Ray: To Instill and Awaken Organizational Skills and Abilities

Begin the Holy Breath. Envision the Auburn ray as the radiant colors of a golden red-orange tree leaf in the Fall. Breathe Spirit and the Auburn Ray in through the nose; breathe negative and/or distracting energies out through the mouth. You may wish to call forth Saint Germaine and the Violet Flame to transform negative energies into love.

We clear the interior environment first. In the same way that computers defragment the hard drive by clearing away clutter and reorganizing, the Auburn Ray cleanses and clears the brain, in order to provide more effective, usable space.

Archangel Zoriel, I invite you and the Auburn Ray into my heart center. Breathe in deeply. Feel the Auburn Ray begin to penetrate.

Continue the Holy Breath. Feel the Auburn warmth embracing you, embracing each cell, each DNA strand, alerting each to the liberation which de-cluttering and organization can bring.

Archangel Zoriel stands with you. You are lovingly enveloped by the Messenger of God.

Embracing, enveloping with warmth, the Auburn Ray comes in through the right side, providing you with the "knack" or gift to see and organize on every level, inner and outer. *Organizing brain cells is not limiting them, but freeing the brain cells, (re)awakening your very DNA to a higher purpose and vision.*

Rest in the Auburn Ray at this time, continuing to use the Holy Breath. Firing up the connecting synapses, the Auburn Ray offers your brain a rejuvenation treatment. Take your brain to the spa!

Continue to rest and allow the inner healing. Archangel Zoriel continues to inspect and reactivate each aspect; each cell in the brain, radiating in the entire body, especially the heart. The Auburn Ray travels, embraces and rejuvenates.

All of our cells add up collectively to an inner vision. The Auburn Ray clears and reactivates the DNA in each and every cell. Where there is emotional/mental/physical road grime spattering a cell, the Auburn Ray acts as a super windshield cleaner, exposing clarity and unobstructed views, guided by Divine perspective.

Each cell works with the others, collectively vibrating with reactivated DNA, helping you intensify and clear your inner vision, and set your goals. The cells may discover and identify the need for another particular ray and healing—for example, from the Flame Orange Ray for the Healing of Shame, Indignity and Humiliation with Archangel Jophiel.

With this clarity of inner vision, each cell now focuses on what is needed from other Divine healing rays. Clear inner vision and goals for healing are established.

Time and energy are also crucial areas where organization is needed in order to allow personal liberation.

Continue the Holy Breath. Direct the Auburn Ray to your hands. Feel your hands get warm as the Auburn Ray works with you and through you. Your hands now radiate the warmth and power of the Auburn Ray and the Messenger of God. Feel the Divine power of the Auburn light streaming out of your hands.

Put your hands on your heart, and feel the Auburn Ray radiating warmth. *Where do I <u>desire</u> to spend my time and energy?* Ask this question as the Auburn Ray radiates into your heart, clearing energies. Write down the answers. Keep it simple. No need to psychoanalyze, just listen to your heart and write your heart's desire.

Continue the Holy Breath, your radiant hands placed over your heart. With Archangel Zoriel and the Auburn Ray, inquire: *Where do I **need** to spend my time and energies?* Listen to the answers emanating from your heart, and write.

Continue to breathe the Holy Breath; continue to radiate the Auburn Ray into your heart with your hands. Hands on heart, compare the written *need* and *heart's desire* lists. Ask Archangel Zoriel and the Auburn Ray to align your needs and your heart's desire.

Each reawakened cell and DNA seeks the others; and collectively, all cells work together to establish the goals for your heart's desire and *what you need* to do. Invite your rejuvenated and reorganized brain cells, again with the Auburn Ray, to map a simple schedule which will include both the heart's desire and needs.

Go forward with the list. If confusion or frustrations occur, enjoy a deep breath, call in Archangel Zoriel and ask for the Auburn Ray to clarify, to once again rejuvenate and reorganize. Use the Holy Breath at any moment.

As you feel the interior healing complete, let us turn to the exterior.

The Auburn Ray has another important purpose: to help you clear your environment of the clutter and stuff which imprisons you. Use the Holy Breath.

Call forth the Auburn Ray again to assist you to see, feel, and consider the objects around you. How are you being served? How are you not being served?

Once again, feel the Auburn Light streaming from your hands. Pick up any object in your environment, allow the Auburn Ray to emanate from your hands, and choose.

Is this thing serving you? Do you truly need this? Is it your heart's desire to keep this? If the answer is no, bless the object and release it—sell, give or toss away, as appropriate.

Use the Auburn Ray in this manner to clear and clean your home environment. Distill your belongings with essentials remaining. Instill liberation. Start in a small area—your bedroom, perhaps, or even corner of your bedroom, or a drawer or closet. Follow this procedure in each of your physical environments. You will soon be free. Archangel Zoriel, with the Auburn Ray, delightfully awaits your invitation, and loves to visit often.

Closing Affirmation

On winged feet of liberation, I dance lightly and joyfully upon the path of light, unburdened by inner and outer clutter. I AM free. I AM liberated. I AM all that I need. I AM perfect inner vision. I attract into my life only that which is my heart's desire. I attract into my life only that which serves me, and I release all inner and outer clutter which does not serve me. I have all the time that I need. I AM all the energy which I need.

Closing Prayer

Beloved Spirit, as newly cleaned windows allow the light to penetrate without shadow or obstruction, I AM fresh, clean and reawakened, allowing all Divine light to infuse each cell and DNA in my being.

Guide me to be aware of which healing rays and Divine Partners are most beneficial to me in this moment of readiness. Help me to continue to be open to receive the healing energies as they are offered by our heavenly Friends, and to notice that my Friends are on perpetual standby, awaiting my invitation. Help me to continue to discern what is important to me, and to notice where my energies and time are given. I am thankful for this miraculous healing, and the magical doors and windows which are opening to me, even in this moment.

Author's note: The instant and powerful warmth of the Auburn Ray generated a physical heat and pulsating in my hands and heart, which I found immensely encouraging.

I especially enjoyed the creating the lists with Archangel Zoriel, with my hands radiating powerful, continuous heat over my heart, helping me to notice my own One-ness with Spirit and gifting me with a practical, conscious demonstration from Archangel Zoriel. I knew I was enfolded in His wings.

I started this meditation with an awful sense of being

weighted down with situations and tasks at hand.

    Divinely inspired from my heart, my heart's desire and "need" lists allowed me to form a solid basis for a Divinely inspired schedule, to help me out of the "stuck" I was in and to move forward. Such practicality in the company of Archangels!

    The Auburn Ray has given me hope, and an enormous feeling of personal relief, which I did not expect.

Chapter Fifteen

Aquamarine Ray of Gentility and Grace
Used in partnership to smooth and make more gentle the experience of other healing rays.

Lady Quan Yin, Divine Goddess of Mercy, Compassion and Charity

Enhancement!

Opening Affirmation
Bathed in gentility and grace I AM.
Perfectly prepared, in all four bodies, for further healing I AM.

Opening Prayer
As I prepare to courageously embark upon my journey of even further healing. I invite you, Lady Quan Yin, Divine Goddess of Mercy, Compassion and Charity, and the Aquamarine Ray to prepare my being in all four bodies for further healing with other Divine healing rays. I ask for the Divine liquid Aquamarine Light, under your direction, to bathe, reactivate, and encompass each DNA strand, each cell within my human form with Aquamarine gentility and grace. I invite your energies and the Aquamarine Ray to prepare me fully for the intensity of the next healing ray, that I more fully and gently receive the healing experience.

Invitation and Permission
I invite Lady Quan Yin and the Aquamarine Ray of Gentility and Grace into my heart, my soul, and all four bodies. I give my

permission to fully allow Lady Quan Yin to direct the Aquamarine Ray to any part of all four bodies where it is most needed. I allow the Divine Aquamarine Light to reawaken the DNA in my physical body.

Beloveds! Let us make more gentle the experience when using the more intense Divine healing rays, such as the Platinum Ray. ***More gentle does not mean less powerful.*** Not diminished, the healings of intense Divine healing rays *are made even stronger and more effective as the Aquamarine energies prepare and allow all four bodies to more readily, more fully and more gently receive the Divine healing rays.*

Lady Quan Yin directs the Aquamarine Ray to bathe and prepare each of your cells, each DNA strand, to more gently and comfortably receive the next, more intense, healing ray of your choice.

By lessening your conscious *experience* of intensity, the benefits of intense healing rays are more fully allowed and enhanced.

Let us begin. Seek your sacred space. Begin the Holy Breath. You deserve this time with Spirit. *Honor and trust yourself and Spirit to make the clear and complete connection.*

Lady Quan Yin, Divine Goddess of Mercy, Compassion and Charity, I invite you and the Aquamarine Ray of Gentility and Grace to prepare me for further healing rays. I AM worthy to receive Divine healing, to experience even more deeply my connection to Spirit.

Envision a brilliant tropical beach. The water is Aquamarine, almost turquoise, warm and inviting. You are ready, even longing, for the warmth and joy of the experience.

Continue the Holy Breath. As light and warmth penetrate and make radiant the water, so the glistening liquid light of the Aquamarine Ray of Gentility and Grace lights, penetrates and bathes your entire being, every cell, every DNA strand, in all four bodies. All aspects of your being are infused with Divine, unconditional love and Aquamarine Light.

In the heart, the Aquamarine Liquid Light shimmers, pausing, searching. Most hearts have a great longing for healing. Lovingly, the Aquamarine Ray embraces, with grace and gentility, each wounded and healthy cell and DNA strand, preparing the way for further, more intense healing rays.

The Aquamarine Light rests as long as needed in the heart, expanding into the brain, preparing the eyes, the ears, the throat.

Continue the Holy Breath. The Aquamarine Ray expands from the heart to the solar plexus, lighting, enveloping, strengthening.

The liquid, shimmering light, under the Divine and loving guidance of Lady Quan Yin, continues to expand, seeking and bathing each aspect in all four bodies in liquid, Aquamarine Light.

Continue the Holy Breath. Lady Quan Yin and the Aquamarine Radiance have bathed every DNA strand in your entire being in a shimmering, soft liquid cloak, *to more gently receive and thereby enhance the effectiveness* of even the most intense Divine healing ray. A gentle, powerful partnership, you might say, between healing rays and Holy Friends to serve you.

Call forth Lady Quan Yin and the Aquamarine Ray of Gentility and Grace first to enhance, in harmonious partnership, other more intense healing rays, to make more gentle the experience of healing.

Closing Affirmation
My inner and outer being is radiant with gentility and grace.

I AM cloaked in Aquamarine Light, within and without, now perfectly prepared and ready to receive further healing.

Closing Prayer

I offer a prayer of thanks for the present and future healings I experience, and for the gentle Aquamarine energies which prepare the way, making my experience with the next, more intense healing ray more gentle. I offer my intention and prayer to receive the fullest benefits from both the Aquamarine Ray of Gentility and Grace, and the more intense healing ray which follows.

Author's note: Once more, Lady Quan Yin's energies seemed to arrive in my heart area, and radiated outwards, expanding through my throat and my head, with a great feeling of warmth. I also initially experienced subtle warmth on my right side. I was especially conscious of the energies in my heart and solar plexus areas.

Chapter Sixteen

Royal Deep Blue Ray of Peace and Prosperity
Archangel Michael, Archangel of Truth and Healing

*Your peace and prosperity belong to you.
In order to allow peace and manifest prosperity,
we must be clear, beloveds,
about what we need and our heart's desire.*

Opening Affirmation

I AM deserving of Divine abundance and Divine peace. Divine peace and Divine prosperity are harmoniously and gloriously aligned within me.

Opening Prayer

Within my very soul, I desire and intend the Divine harmony of clarity, radiant prosperity and sweet, Divine peace in all aspects of my life. I offer my availability, my willingness, and every particle of faith, hope and trust I have, to Spirit and Archangel Michael. Realign and restore within me the perfect awareness of the continuous Divine dance of the these great gifts, peace and prosperity.

Invitation and Permission

I invite Archangel Michael and the Royal Blue Ray of Peace and Prosperity into my heart, my soul, and all four bodies. I give my permission to fully allow Archangel Michael to direct the Royal Blue Light to any part of all four bodies where it is most needed. I allow the Royal Blue Light to reawaken the DNA in my physical body.

Beloveds, it is not necessary to give up peace in order to find prosperity. Nor is it necessary to give up prosperity to find peace. Prosperity and peace, in all four bodies—spiritual, mental, emotional and physical, are, in fact, perfectly, Divinely aligned. *You can have it all.*

Archangel Michael and the Royal Blue Ray *(re)align each cell, to the very DNA strand, to accept and enjoy both peace and prosperity in harmony, in perfect alignment.* Seek your sacred space. This is your time. You do not owe a debt, physical, spiritual, emotional or mental, to anyone. Your every moment spent in stillness with Spirit is precious and valuable.

Begin the Holy Breath. I invite Archangel Michael, Archangel of Truth and Healing, and the Royal Blue Ray of Peace and Prosperity into my heart, my soul, all four bodies. Envision a bright, Royal Blue flag, billowing in the air. Look closely: notice your name written in Golden Light upon the Royal Blue Flag. Archangel Michael is your Champion.

Continue the Holy Breath. Archangel Michael is with you now, with the Royal Blue Ray of Peace and Prosperity, surrounding, healing your being in Royal Blue Light.

Continue the Holy Breath. Focus on the physical, mental, emotional and spiritual bodies. *Reawaken and realign my very DNA, Archangel Michael, to resonate and align with sweet, Divine peace and abundant prosperity. Willing, worthy and available I AM to receive and manifest peace and prosperity in my* **mental body**. *Willing, worthy and available I AM to receive and manifest peace and prosperity in my* **emotional body**.

*Willing, worthy and available I AM to receive and manifest peace and prosperity in my **physical body**. Willing, worthy and available I AM to receive and manifest peace and prosperity in my **spiritual body**.*

Let us reconcile, manifest and enjoy the Divine gifts of prosperity and peace. Archangel Michael and the Royal Blue Ray are healing the great illusion blocking peace and prosperity; the illusion of "I don't deserve it."

The Royal Blue Ray, like a series of brilliant, electric arcs of Royal Blue Light, approaches your right side, penetrating each individual aspect of the brain, seeking, discovering those darkened cells and DNA strands. Some DNA strands are hiding, and some are calling for revival of life and light.

Continue the Holy Breath. Archangel Michael and the Royal Blue Ray, with vibrant, electric arcs of Royal Blue Light, electrify each of these cells and DNA strands back to life, to Divine Light. Each of these dark spaces, which has been taught unworthiness beliefs, has been waiting for a long, long time to be noticed, shocked and resurrected, back to life and to vitality.

I deserve and I allow Divine peace and Divine prosperity. Affirm out loud, beloveds, even if you are not convinced. *I deserve and I allow Divine peace and Divine prosperity in all four bodies.*

Continue the Holy Breath as Archangel Michael continues to work in the brain, and moves the electric arcs of Royal Blue Light throughout the head, down through the throat, radiating, expanding to the heart, expanding throughout the body.

Continue the Holy Breath. Once again, electric arcs of Royal Blue Light seek, in the heart, those areas which have been wounded.

Each DNA strand in the heart is re-alerted, revived, reawakened, healed as the electric arcs of the Royal Blue Ray reveal the truth.

Archangel Michael guides the Royal Blue Ray down the body, the arms, to the finger tips, the solar plexus.

Continue the Holy Breath. The Blue arcing lights are resting, seeking in the solar plexus, in each internal organ, now, those cells and DNA strands awaiting the resurrection, the healing with the dazzling Light of the Royal Blue Healing Ray.

Continue the Holy Breath. Breathe in the Royal Blue Light. Archangel Michael and the Royal Blue Ray leave a luminous path, continuing down the body, the abdomen, the legs, to the bottoms of your feet, pausing, healing with special attention where needed.

Continue the Holy Breath. Continue to rest as Archangel Michael guides the Royal Blue Light, perfectly aligning the energies of peace and prosperity. Spirit intends abundance. Your cells and DNA strands are perfectly healed, radiant in the light, perfectly aligned to accept and enjoy, in abundant harmony, peace and prosperity.

Closing Affirmation
Peace and prosperity dance and rejoice in flourishing partnership in my life. I AM sweet Divine peace and endlessly abundant prosperity.

Closing Prayer
Reconciled within me, Divinely radiant, and deserving as I AM, I can now enjoy both Divine peace and Divine prosperity in perfect harmony in all four bodies. I heartily thank Spirit and Archangel Michael for my Divine ability to open and receive these gifts and the healing of their alignment within me. I AM grateful to enjoy and to notice peace within me, without beginning and without end, and prosperity, without beginning and without end.

Author's note: I sensed the warmth of the Royal Blue Ray on my right side, and strongly felt the energies of Archangel Michael and the Royal Blue Ray in my heart and solar plexus area.

Chapter Seventeen

Chartreuse Ray: An Opportunity to Go Deeper Into Discernment
Archangel Michael, Archangel of Truth and Healing

Go deeper to go forward.
Move deeper into discernment,
in order to move on.
Discern what is in order to create what will be.

Opening Affirmation
I AM ready to be liberated from the strings of illusion.
I AM willing to be willing to more deeply, more Divinely, discern the truth.

Opening Prayer
I come to you, Spirit, with the deep soul desire to be liberated from the strings of attachment to illusion, to be freed completely from resistance to the truth. I proclaim my intention, Spirit, to move forward with an accelerated speed in my life. I know that to move forward, I need to cultivate and use my Divine ability to more deeply discern the truth. I intend this healing with Archangel Michael to be profound and complete. I intend to clearly, deeply, Divinely discern what is, so that I can create and manifest my deep Divine soul vision of what of what will be.

Invitation and Permission

I invite Archangel Michael and the Chartreuse Ray to go Deeper into Discernment into my heart, my soul, and all four bodies. I give my permission to fully allow Archangel Michael to direct the Chartreuse Light to any part of all four bodies where it is most needed. I allow the Chartreuse Light to reawaken the DNA in my physical body.

Beloveds, this is Archangel Michael. I AM here with my Blue Sword of Truth to cut away those strings binding you to illusion, to denial, to any energies which are false, which hold you back and imprison your true nature.

Be fully aware of the value of being aware, of the importance of clarity, of the value of the ability and the willingness to Divinely discern what is.

Truth and the ability to discern the truth are essential, central to your well being and your life on this planet.

Any attachment to falsehood can only bring you negative results. Your very DNA must be reactivated to reawaken hope, clarity, the cutting away of illusion and the ability and willingness to discern.

Find your sacred space, get comfortable, relax. Begin the Holy Breath.

Once again, beloveds, we remind you that when you find yourself in any immediate need to discern the truth, begin the Holy Breath, right where you are standing. Call forth Archangel Michael and the Chartreuse Ray for the Discernment of Truth. A moment, a thought, a Holy Breath, and a brief prayer is all it takes to get your Celestial Warrior on board instantly. Archangel Michael awaits your invitation.

Archangel Michael, I call you forth in this moment, with the Chartreuse Ray for Deeper Discernment of Truth. In the very moment of your invitation, Archangel Michael and the Chartreuse Ray radiantly enfold you.

Chartreuse Ray: An Opportunity To Go Deeper into Discernment

Envision the Chartreuse Ray as a funnel of radiant Chartreuse Light, entering near the top of your head. Your fingers and temples may pulsate with the intensity of the brilliant, Chartreuse Light.

Continue to breathe. The Chartreuse Ray, carefully guided by Archangel Michael, begins its holy work in the brain, to move you deeper, more immediately, into discernment.

As you breathe, the Chartreuse Ray continues to spin. Think of the brilliant Chartreuse Light as a Divine weed whacker.

Spinning, now, the Chartreuse Light seeks each cell, each DNA strand where the strings of attachment to illusion have become a convenient habit.

Continue the Holy Breath. Your cells and DNA strands are being freed by the Chartreuse Ray, as the brilliantly spinning light is cutting away the strings of attachment to illusion. Once liberated, the DNA strands and cells are (re)awakened, infused with the Divine knowledge, with Divine discernment of the truth by Archangel Michael.

Continue the Holy Breath. The cells and DNA strands are being re-alerted, electrified by Archangel Michael and the vibrant light of the Chartreuse Ray back into their original, natural state: *seek* the truth, *discern* the truth, use the *Divine Holy Light* and knowledge to discern what is true.

The vibrant Chartreuse Light continues in the brain. The cells and DNA strands relearn deep discernment of the truth, without the filters of illusion.

Envision each cell inside its own individual, loving funnel of Chartreuse Light. The funnel continues to embrace and envelop each brain cell and DNA strand, healing, healing. The Chartreuse Ray continues through the brain, embracing and enveloping each cell.

Continue the Holy Breath. Your first response, now, is the deep discernment of the truth. The habit of the attachment to illusion as an immediate response has been cleared, and as the healing energies integrate, this habit is dissolved and is no more.

Continue to breathe. The Chartreuse Ray radiates to the eyes, the ears, the mouth, and the throat. The Chartreuse Light is moving down, seeking, surgically cutting away the strings of attachment to illusion, to false perceptions.

Radiating to the heart, the gleaming Chartreuse Ray pauses. It is in the heart, beloveds, as well as in the brain, where it is essential for us to understand the truth of what is going on around us. Without the discernment of the truth, we make choices reacting to an illusion, a falsehood. As you know, beloveds, this attachment to illusion does not serve you, and may result in hurt and harm.

The vibrant, shimmering light of the Chartreuse Ray embraces the heart, where so much truth, as well as illusion, lives. More gently now, the Chartreuse Light seeks each cell and DNA strand, enhancing those which are radiant with the discernment of truth, cutting the strings of illusion from those which need liberation. Each cell and DNA strand is individually embraced, Divinely reawakened and Divinely altered, by the Chartreuse Light.

Continue the Holy Breath. The entire heart is embraced as one, with the brilliant Chartreuse ray, spinning, spinning, clearing and embracing.

The Chartreuse Ray pauses here, for this holy clearing of your precious, your Divine heart. Archangel Michael is loving and gentle, completing the healing in your heart.

Moving down to the solar plexus, all the internal organs, the Chartreuse Ray continues. Continue the Holy Breath.

The Light illuminates all the way down to the feet, where each visible footstep is accompanied by the invisible footsteps of Spirit and angels, clearing the path to a deeper discernment.

Look down at your feet. Previous webs of attachment, entangling you and slowing you down, have disappeared and been obliterated. Each step you take on the path of light is liberated, free, and discerning, accompanied by beloved, connected friends from heaven, by the I AM Light.

The healing energies will take several days to integrate within all four of your bodies. Archangel Michael awaits your next invitation, in a moment, a thought, a prayer. As your champion, He is poised, Sword of Truth ready, ever standing by, to reawaken even deeper discernment to serve you.

Closing Affirmation
Without illusion, I more deeply discern what is. As I discern the truth of what is, I create and manifest my own Divinely inspired intention and vision of what will be.

Closing Prayer
I am grateful to Spirit, to Archangel Michael for this healing, this liberation from attachment to illusion. As I move deeper into discernment, both human and Divine, I achieve more clarity, more courage, more Divine inspiration to create my true heart's desires and intentions. Accompany me, Spirit, upon this magnificent journey of transformation, of the deeper discernment of what is. Inspire me Divinely to discern the truth that there are no limits to what can be, as I more deeply discern all that is within me, all that the Divine offers, all that is possible.

Author's note: I felt heat and energy at the back, almost top of my head, and a warmth around the right side of my head and face. As Chartreuse energies seemed to move down along my neck, I had a strong sense of the energies across my shoulders, to the heart area. I could feel my fingertips and hands pulse. I also had the sense of the mildest electrical charge, all the way down to the soles of my feet, part way through the meditation. Heat emanating from my the palms of my hands was also part of this experience.

Chapter Eighteen

Blue Ray: Truth, Justice, Clarity, Healing, and Hope (Divine Confidence)
Archangel Michael, Archangel of Truth and Healing

*Seek any one energy
and the other energies follow.
Let's slice and dice away the illusion, the
extraneous, to discover and fully express and
manifest Divine gifts and realities.*

Opening Prayer

*Beloved Spirit and Archangel Michael, with Your Divine Blue Light, restore within me Divine hope, radiant and bright, where my hope has faded and been battered by discouragement. Divinely accompany me as I seek to be both Divinely just and the voice of justice. Replace within me confusion, doubt or illusion, with Divine discernment, that I may know truth and clarity, the **co-fusion** of the Divine, and act and speak on behalf of justice and compassion. I intend my clarity to be crystal clear and Divine. Let my voice, intoned with clarity, justice, truth, compassion and hope, be the healing voice to myself, in all four bodies, and to those around me.*

Opening Affirmation
Radiant hope, Divine and abundant,
is restored within me.
I seek and discern the truth, and I know crystal clear clarity.
Discerning the Divine truth,
I think and act not with judgment, but with justice.
I have a Divine awareness to mind my own business.

Invitation and Permission
I invite Archangel Michael and the Blue Ray of Truth, Justice, Healing, Hope and Clarity into my heart, my soul, and all four bodies. I give my permission to fully allow Archangel Michael to direct the Blue Light to any part of all four bodies where it is most needed. I allow the Blue Light to reawaken the DNA in my physical body.

Greetings and welcome, beloved friends. The energies of Truth, Justice, Healing, Hope and Clarity are Divine integrated energies— the awesome fivesome. Once more, as with other groups of Divine energies, when one energy manifests and expresses, all four of the others (and more) also manifest and express.

Where truth is present, hope and healing are also present. Within the vitality of truth, hope and healing, justice and clarity flourish. These Divine energies are *never separate* from one another.

Seek your sacred space. Begin the Holy Breath. Archangel Michael, I invite You with the Blue Ray of Truth, Justice, Healing, Hope and Clarity into my mental, physical, emotional and spiritual bodies. Envision the sun dancing upon the deep blue sea, creating brilliant reflections of light. Such is the brilliant, vibrant, deep Blue Ray of Archangel Michael.

The healing by Archangel Michael and the Blue Ray accelerates the awareness and events in your life which move you forward. The joy of healing with this ray is the power of the combination of these five Divine energies.

Continue the Holy breath. The Blue Light enters your heart center, offering a heat and energy around the back of your head as Archangel Michael and the Divine energies begin their holy work.

The radiant Blue Light radiates through the brain, reactivating, bathing, enveloping each cell and each DNA strand, in the brilliant Blue Light, restoring equilibrium, healing distortion, restoring the balanced view, the balanced perspective. Within Divine balance and perspective, truth, justice, clarity, healing and hope thrive and radiate into all aspects of all four bodies.

Continue to breathe. Archangel Michael, with his Blue Sword of Truth, is slicing and dicing away the illusions and attachments which imprison us in all four bodies.

Making decisions and taking action based on illusion and distortion are like trying to run through mud. The journey is arduous, and the arrival to your destination is woefully delayed or cut off completely.

When, beloveds, you view the truth through the Divine lens of justice and clarity, through hope, you skyrocket forward, with hope as your traveling companion.

Continue to breathe. *Justice I AM. Balanced I AM. The perspective of Justice, Hope and Truth, I AM. I AM ready to move forward!*

Continue the Holy Breath as the Blue Ray continues to expand. The glowing Blue Ray, vibrant with Archangel Michael's guidance, continues towards the eyes to see, the ears to listen, all with Divine perspective of truth, hope and justice, resonating with clarity.

As illusion continues to be separated from truth, the healing continues, restoring hope, restoring the Divine perspective and balance.

Continue to breathe. Energizing, revitalizing, reactivating, clearing and cleansing, the vivid Blue Light continues: to the mouth, where truth is spoken, with the intonement of hope. The truth always arrives with the energy of hope, of clarification, of healing.

The vivid Blue Light continues to the throat—where the truth is spoken, not the illusion. The willingness to discern and the ability to speak the truth is reactivated. Justice and Hope encompass our thoughts and intone our words. Clarity is allowed and achieved.

Your are energized--notice the tingling as the DNA and cells are reminded, reactivated, renewed with hope, truth, and the perspective of justice.

Continue the Holy Breath. The Blue Light, beloveds, has been loving and radiating within your heart since the start of this meditation. You are Divinely protected and Divinely supported in this and all moments.

It is in the heart, beloveds, where attachment to illusion may be strongest. Once more, Archangel Michael carefully performs micro or major laser surgery, depending on the strength of the attachment, to free the heart.

The Blue Light envelops the heart. You may have a physical sensation in your heart area as Archangel Michael and the Blue Ray liberate the heart, healing distortion, restoring hope, healing, and the just perspective, so critical to each of our lives! Once again, each cell and DNA strand is reactivated, bathed, enveloped, healed by the holy Blue Light energies. Once more, clarity emerges.

Continue the Holy Breath, beloveds. You are enfolded in Archangel Michael's wings. Breathe. The Blue Ray of Truth, Justice, Healing, Hope and Clarity continues to heal and restore.

Radiating, restoring, vibrant Blue Light continues to expand, refreshing, restoring, and revitalizing all cells and DNA strands, traveling down the solar plexus and internal organs.

Continue the Holy Breath. By reawakening and revitalizing, Archangel Michael restores balance, perspective, and especially truth, hope, healing, and justice.

Archangel Michael awaits your invitation in any moment, wherever you are, whatever your circumstances. Invite Him, and He is instantly with you.

Closing Affirmation

The Divine energies of truth, justice, healing and hope are my Divine tool kit to create clarity.

Closing Prayer

Help me, Spirit, to use my Divine tool kit of truth, justice, healing, hope and clarity in very moment of need. I intend clarity. As I AM healed, let my voice be the voice of healing, truth and justice, instilling and reawakening hope. I intend every thought, every considered action and inaction to be cloaked in the Blue Light of Healing, Truth, Justice, Clarity, and Hope; each breath and moment surrounded and grounded in the compassion and unconditional love of the Divine. Help me to guard against self righteousness and overzealousness. In seeing the truth, in knowing clarity, I offer healing, hope and justice, to myself and others, and to all conditions on this planet. I intend to be ever vigilant, guarding against judgment, not mistaking judgment for discernment. I heartily thank you, Archangel Michael, for restoring and reactivating truth, justice, healing, hope, and clarity in my heart and in my mental, physical, emotional and spiritual bodies.

Author's note: Archangel Michael's energies seem to arrive around the back of my head, and radiate across my shoulders, down my arms. I could sense the Blue Ray energies in my hands. I also felt the energies in my heart—almost a sense of butterflies. My hands felt expanded, elevated in energy, and I could feel the heat radiating outwards from my palms.

Chapter Nineteen

Sky Blue Ray of Truth and Hope, Faith, Courage and Clarity
Archangel Michael, Archangel of Truth and Healing

You need to discern the truth to activate hope. Hope is activated by truth <u>and</u> clarity.

> Sky Blue Ray enfold me
> Sky Blue Ray surround me
> Sky Blue Ray infuse me
> Sky Blue Ray diffuse throughout me

Opening Affirmation
Generous I AM in my own spirit, to be open to know and receive the truth and allow crystal clear clarity. My faith, hope, courage and clarity are reactivated.

Opening Prayer
*Beloved Spirit and Archangel Michael, my prayer is to discern the truth, that I can know the hope. Clear and replace any confusion I have with **co-fusion** of truth, faith, trust, courage and hope and clarity. I intend to be Divinely generous in my own spirit, to open to know and receive the truth. My prayer is for the Divine generosity of Spirit and Archangel Michael, to prepare, guide and support me in my discernment of the truth, and to*

inspire Divine courage, faith and clarity as I walk the path of action which follows discernment. I invite Archangel Michael and the Divine Sky Blue Ray to heal me in all four bodies, to Divinely reawaken and alter my DNA to resonate with the energies of the discernment of truth, faith, hope, courage and clarity.

Invitation and Permission
I invite Archangel Michael and the Sky Blue Ray of Truth and Hope, Faith, Courage and Clarity, into my heart, my soul, and all four bodies. I give my permission to fully allow Archangel Michael to direct the Sky Blue Light to any part of all four bodies where it is most needed. I allow the Sky Blue Light to reawaken the DNA in my physical body.

Beloveds! Archangel Michael is present, and he is unsheathing his Sword of Truth and Justice. What a powerful, loving friend each of you have with Archangel Michael, ever ready to be with you, in any moment of your invitation.

You might feel in this moment an aching in your heart—this is the hopelessness rising, looking for a healing.

You might feel a sensation of your heart beating, or a weight in your chest—again the hopelessness is rising, seeking hope, looking for Archangel Michael and the Sky Blue Ray of Truth and Hope. Within the energies of truth and hope, faith, courage and clarity are also reactivated and integrated. Each energy activates the other.

Let us begin. Archangel Michael is already near you, awaiting your invitation.

Seek your sacred space. Begin the Holy Breath. In through the nose, out through the mouth. Envision the brightest, bluest sky at which you have ever marveled. Archangel Michael brings an even more intense Sky Blue Light to you in this moment.

Archangel Michael, I call you forth to guide this healing. I call forth the Sky Blue Ray of Truth and Hope. Archangel

Michael is with you instantly.

Continue the Holy Breath. Sky Blue Ray enfold me. Sky Blue Ray surround me. Sky Blue Ray infuse me. Sky Blue Ray diffuse throughout me.

Feel yourself being elevated by the Sky Blue Ray energies.

Archangel Michael, I invite you and give you full, energetic permission to gift me with the Sky Blue Ray, to physically alter, unlock and reactivate the DNA within me that I may *discern the truth and know the hope, that my every thought, every breath, every action is imbued with faith, courage, and clarity.*

Continue to breathe. With each breath, you breathe in the Sky Blue Light. The Sky Blue Ray enters mostly on the right side. Continue to focus on Archangel Michael and the Sky Blue Ray, as you continue the Holy Breath.

Sky Blue Ray, enfold me, surround me, infuse me, diffuse within me.

Rest. Allow. Do not think that you must compel, or try. Only allow. As you are enfolded and surrounded by the Sky Blue Ray, breathe in the Sky Blue Light.

As you breathe in the Sky Blue Ray, the energies of discernment of truth, hope, faith, courage and clarity are integrating within you. Breathe out the energies of hopelessness and illusion.

Your head might begin to pulse as the Sky Blue Ray works within the brain cells; the eyes, the ears, the throat. You see, hear, listen and speak the truth, infilling with the energies of hope, faith, courage, and clarity.

Continue to breathe. Archangel Michael is seeking the illusion, the false beliefs imprisoning hope and truth in each cell, in each DNA strand.

Continue to breathe. Archangel Michael, with the piercing Sky Blue Light, is bathing each cell, each DNA strand in

Sky Blue Light. He is using his sword to cut away the dark crust which covers cells in judgment and darkness.

Allow the Sky Blue Ray to rest there as long is it takes for Archangel Michael to clear, cleanse, and physically reactivate your cells and DNA strands with truth and hope.

Continue to breathe. Each cell, each DNA strand in your brain, now, is brightly lit, cleansed, radiating hope and the discernment of truth.

Continue to breathe. The Sky Blue Ray is moving and working in your heart. You might also feel the Sky Blue Ray radiating both into and from the palms of your hands.

As the Sky Blue Light pauses in the heart, DNA strands and darkened cells are rising to meet Archangel Michael, longing for the release into truth and hope.

Continue the Holy Breath. Here in the heart, beloveds, you may feel flutters, butterflies, as these darkened cells and DNA strands rise to the light. Archangel Michael is very busy in this moment, in your heart: healing, reactivating truth and hope in each the DNA strand and cell.

In your heart, beloveds, hope lives, and hopelessness can slyly stow away. Your champion Archangel Michael displaces the hopelessness with hope. Each cell, each DNA strand is lovingly and powerfully resurrected and healed with Sky Blue Light.

Continue the Holy Breath as this holy work takes place, releasing illusion and hopelessness which have been held in the heart for so long. Continue the Holy Breath. I release, I release I release.

Illusion and hopelessness live together—one needs the other to survive. Archangel Michael continues to replace hopelessness with hope, to replace illusion with truth, even where resistance is met.

Allow the Sky Blue Ray to continue its work, releasing, transmuting, activating, awakening.

Continue the Holy Breath.

Sky Blue Ray of Truth and Hope, Faith, Courage and Clarity

The Sky Blue Ray continues down the body, seeking each cell, each DNA strand, down the solar plexus, into each internal organ, restoring light, restoring, health, restoring hope, restoring truth and discernment of truth.

The Sky Blue Ray continues all the way down to the soles of your feet, grounding you in clarity, hope and discernment.

When you feel complete, express your gratitude.

This Sky Blue Ray is available at any moment, and can be used in one moment or a longer session of meditation.

Your heart, your mind, are free to see the truth and to know hope.

When you see the truth of a condition, situation, environment, or relationship, you are released from indecision, inaction, resistance. *Co-fusion* of truth and hope replace confusion. Clarity surfaces; the course becomes clear. Choose: is it better to dance in the light, or to stumble around in the dark?

Once the clear course is set, the natural consequence is to be filled with, and to radiate, hope and courage. The clarity and direction of the course are filled completely with the light of Spirit. Therein resides the hope, the truth, courage and clarity. Faith thrives within you.

Closing Affirmation
I discern and I AM truth and clarity.
Living, radiant hope and courage I AM.

Closing Prayer
I thank Spirit, Archangel Michael and the Sky Blue Ray. Spirit, guide me to continue to discern my clear course of action Divinely lit before me. My footsteps radiate Divine courage, energy, hope and clarity. I know where I am going and why, and each step is guided by Divine clarity and faith.

Author's note: The first experience upon beginning the Holy Breath was a fluttering sensation in my heart area, followed by a sense of pulsating in my fingertips. Energies seem to arrive around the crown. I had a strong sense that the back of my head was being held, cradled, by Archangel Michael and the Sky Blue energies.

The warm energies seemed to rest a long while around my neck and into my upper back, then seemed to radiate across my shoulders. I wonder if this has something to do with strengthening and healing those areas where we carry burdens, and with the release of the burdens as we achieve clarity.

The energies then seemed to radiate across my shoulders down to my arms, down to my hands, where I had a strong sense of a Divine heat and Divine energies emanating from my palms.

Almost at the same time, the energies seemed to go to my heart area, and remain there where I felt a sense of butterflies while the Sky Blue Ray was radiating within me. The energies then seemed to radiate throughout my upper and lower body, traveling all the way down to the soles of my feet, which I could actually feel pulsating.

Chapter Twenty

Magenta Ray of Purity and Hope
Archangel Uriel,
Archangel of Transformation

*Transforming and transmuting
negative into positive.*

*Keep the inner life alive and alert:
spiritual, mental, emotional,
to help the outer physical
to be vibrant and robust.*

Receive wondrous attention.

Opening Affirmation
*As the sun overflows with heat and light,
I overflow with hope and purity.
Hope in abundance I AM. Radiant purity, I AM.*

Opening Prayer
By your Divine love and Divine light, Precious Spirit, hopelessness and fear are replaced by hope and vibrant, constant courage. I know that your gift of healing is mine in a breath, a moment, a thought, a prayer. Archangel Uriel, I invite you to infuse and heal me with the radiant light of the Magenta Ray. Because your spark of God is a part of me, make me ever aware that in fact, God I AM. I intend, in each moment, to see that

hopelessness is unnecessary, and hope and vibrancy, physical, mental, emotional and spiritual, are mine with simply a breath and a prayer. I open my heart to Archangel Uriel at this time, aware that he awaits my invitation.

Invitation and Permission

I invite Archangel Uriel and the Magenta Ray of Purity and Hope into my heart, my soul, and all four bodies. I give my permission to fully allow Archangel Uriel to direct the Magenta Light to any part of all four bodies where it is most needed. I allow the Magenta Light to reawaken the DNA in my physical body.

What is hope, but Divine confidence in the future? What is purity, but the clear, deep, unobstructed connection and access to the Divine? Hope and purity are integrated energies—when you enjoy one, you enjoy the other.

We look to the Magenta Ray of Purity and Hope when we feel beaten by the world, discouraged, beset, undermined, undone, disheartened, flabbergasted.

Think of the Magenta Ray as spiritual resuscitation, offered by Archangel Uriel. The energies of hopelessness are toxic, creating weight around all four of your bodies—pulling everything physical, mental, spiritual and emotional down, in turn, increasing your sense of hopelessness.

To end this cycle and restore hope (Divine confidence), call forth Archangel Uriel and the Magenta Ray of Hope and Purity. Healing and restoration take place in a moment, a breath, a prayer!

Consider the notion of "incoming". Our suit of spiritual shining armor, necessary in all four bodies, is attacked as we are assaulted by negativity, internal or external, in our physical, mental, emotional, even spiritual selves. Despair in one body influences and affects the other bodies. **Do not allow negative** energies of self or others to suck away your life force and vitality.

Our internal glow—our spiritual armor, then becomes tarnished, jagged, even painful. Our being, in all four bodies, is uncomfortable, itchy, distorted.

Consider the texture of your healing. Archangel Uriel and the Magenta Ray of Purity and Hope smooth and transform the jagged edged injuries in your four bodies, the itch, the distortion, in your internal and external spiritual armor. Rough energies of despair are replaced by abundant, smooth flowing hope.

Archangel Uriel guides the Magenta Ray to transform the negative, and through the purifying Magenta Light, wounds are healed and hope is restored.

By strengthening our internal armor; the Magenta Ray helps us to deflect, clear and *transform* the negativity, replacing the sense of helplessness and hopelessness with purity and hope, restoring the smoothness and glow of our internal and external spiritual armor.

When properly tuned and polished with prayer, meditation and compassion, our armor maintains its smoothness, shine and strength.

Seek your sacred space. Begin the Holy Breath. I invite Archangel Uriel and the Magenta Ray of Purity and Hope to meet my soul's desire.

The Magenta Ray comes in through the upper right side. Feel yourself uplifted and lightened in the head and chest as the Magenta Ray expands, transmutes and transforms the negative energies.

Continue the Holy Breath. Rough and sharp edged mental thoughts of unworthiness are transformed into the awareness of this truth. I AM holy. I AM worthy. As Spirit thrives within me, I thrive within Spirit. God I AM.

As a broken bone is x-rayed, treated and mended, Archangel Uriel, directing the Magenta Light, is diagnosing, transforming and healing jagged wounds inflicted by negativity.

Breathe in deeply. Feel the Magenta Ray continuing to warm every aspect of your head your brain. Allow the Magenta Ray to rest in your brain, to transmute, transform and reawaken wounded and sleepy DNA into a smooth, polished, revitalized glow. Magenta light expands, clearing, connecting with Spirit, so that purity and hope (Divine confidence) are expressed in each cell, each molecule, each DNA strand. Down through the brain, the Magenta Ray transforms and heals. Healing the eyes for that which you have beheld; the ears for that which you have heard; the mouth, for the words and thoughts spoken or unspoken; the throat, for the truth rejected or not discerned. The Magenta Ray continues its healing work.

Continue the Holy Breath. If you lose focus, just begin again with the Holy Breath. Allow the healing energies, directed by Archangel Uriel, to continue, rest and heal wherever more time is needed.

Allow time and rest especially when the Magenta Ray reaches your heart, where many injurious energies reside. There may be bleeding and open wounds in the heart, and Archangel Uriel is guiding the Magenta Ray to seek and heal each wound with Divine Magenta Light and Divine unconditional love. The Magenta Ray rests in the heart, discovering, transforming each injury into purity, restoring hope and confidence.

Magenta Ray, rest in my heart, remain here, heal and purify. Restore hope abundantly. Feel the Magenta Light glow in your heart, radiating within and without,
bringing peace and hope to each DNA strand in your body, your heart, your mind, your soul. The hope which is reawakened is simply a resurrection of your natural state.

Archangel Uriel directs the Magenta Ray also to each of your organs: bathing, replenishing, healing, flooding with abundant Divine light each cell, each DNA strand, reawakening, re-energizing, restoring the energies of hope and purity.

Continue the Holy Breath. Feel the Magenta Ray continuing to pulsate throughout our body—down your arms, all the way to your fingertips.

Clearing the path, removing the obstacles of hopelessness, the Magenta Ray deepens our connection and experience of access to God, to Spirit.

Continue the Holy Breath. The Magenta Ray continues to heal, to strengthen, to make once again whole, each body—mental, emotional, physical, spiritual.   In this way, the Magenta Ray heals and transforms the negative energies, making whole, reawakening, and strengthening DNA strands throughout your body, all the way to the soles of your feet. You radiate the Magenta Glow of Hope and Purity with each footstep, with each mental, emotional, spiritual step.

Complete with your own healing, let us consider a global healing.

Envision the Magenta Ray surrounding the planet earth. The Magenta Ray is spinning around our planet, replacing darkness with a deep Magenta Glow. Even a moment with this meditation for the planet has abundant healing results!

Archangel Uriel encourages you to use the Magenta Ray often, and awaits your invitation.

Closing Affirmation

I AM holy. I AM worthy of Divine healing. I AM returned to my natural state of abundant Divine confidence, and perfectly tuned in to the instant access, clear connection to Spirit (purity). I AM strong, powerful, ever present; a part of the ONE.

Closing Prayer

I AM grateful for the restoration of hope and purity. I intend to receive a Divine reminder of the Magenta Ray and all of my spiritual tools at the very moment I may start to feel disheartened. I AM grateful for the spiritual tune up my suits of armor have received in all four bodies, and I intend regular tune-ups with compassion and healing of the Magenta Ray. I intend to recognize my radiance at al times.

Author's note: I felt the Magenta Ray of Hope and Purity come in as a strong warmth on my right side, almost at the back of my head. I had a sense of being made larger—of being magnified as the Magenta ray was working. I could feel my fingertips pulsing, and lightness in my heart

Chapter Twenty-One

Crème Soft White/Soft Yellow Rose Ray
Comfort, Empathy, Consideration and Thoughtfulness
Mother Mary, Queen of Angels

Awareness of our surroundings!
Awareness of how we treat our selves, others, and the surroundings in which we live, work and play.

Opening Affirmation
Hope I AM. Comfort I AM. Radiance I AM.
Love without condition I AM.

Opening Prayer
Mother Mary, Queen of Angels, draw near to me as I invite you and the Crème Soft White/Soft Yellow Rose Ray into my heart and soul in this moment. Surround me with soft rose petals, and infuse me with the fragrance of your Divine roses. Inspire me to offer my own Divine radiance, that I may lift myself and others up; to express my own Divinity, that others are inspired to express theirs, experiencing true Divine confidence and comfort, for ourselves and those we love. As I draw in each breath, help me to breathe in the radiance of God. With every breath I exhale, remind me to offer joy, warmth, and caring, expressing the radiance of God. Mother Mary, Queen of Angels, my intention is to awaken my own Divine discernment, to radiate peace, empathy and comfort, to myself and others.

Invitation and Permission

I invite Mother Mary and the Crème Soft White/Soft Yellow Rose Ray of Comfort, Empathy, Consideration and Thoughtfulness into my heart, my soul, and all four bodies. I give my permission to fully allow Mother Mary to direct the Crème Soft White/Soft Yellow Rose Light to any part of all four bodies where it is most needed. I allow the Crème Soft White/Soft Yellow Rose Light to reawaken the DNA in my physical body.

As Mother Mary is the Queen of Angels, so She is the Queen of Unconditional Love and Comfort. The greatest comfort which can be offered is our Divine unconditional love, with the absence of judgment. We can *empathize*. Empathy lives in the spiritual body—you can not "reason" or emote empathy.

Empathy is not sympathy. Empathy is caring for another with sufficient detachment to act. Sympathy is emotional (sometimes overemotional) engagement (sometimes over-engagement).

We tread in another's sandals only to better imagine, understand and experience a situation, to gain discernment, *without acquiring or taking on* the burdens of another.

In this way, we *discern, not judge*, the experiences of another in order to be of the greatest assistance to the other person.

The Divine comfort does not need to be material. Perhaps the comfort may be a call to prayer or mediation on our own or another person's behalf, or to listen with Divinely inspired responses, spoken or silent, or gestures, which offer comfort to ourselves, or to another.

Let us offer the loving energies of the Crème Soft White/Soft Yellow Rose Ray to ourselves and to those with whom we come into contact—casual or intimate. Divine power thrives in the receiving and the offering of empathy, thoughtfulness and consideration—Divine comfort and unconditional love—to self and others.

    Delight in this opportunity to enjoy your sacred space, and enjoy your healings with the Crème Soft White/Soft Yellow Rose Ray. If you are out and about, remember to create your sacred space, wherever you are, in time of need, with the Holy Breath.

    Begin the Holy Breath. Concentrate on the breath. When your thoughts intrude on your stillness, thank the thoughts, thank the ego, and ask it to move on. Thank you, ego, please move on now. Simply begin again with the Holy Breath.

    Mother Mary, Queen of Angels, I invite you and the Crème Soft White/Soft Yellow Rose Light into my heart in this moment

    Mother Mary encompasses you with Her love. You are already in Her company. Her soft yellow and gentle white roses merge into your heart as she enfolds you within Her arms.

    Envision yourself, face uplifted, enjoying a gentle rain shower of soft yellow and creamy white rose petals shimmering around you. You are in a cloud of radiant soft Yellow Light. Mother Mary, Queen of Angels, is with you.

    Continue to breathe. Feel the gentle Yellow Light—so soft to be nearly yellow but not quite; to be nearly white, but not quite, enter into your heart.

    Gently, the Crème Soft White/Soft Yellow Rose Ray, powerful yet most gentle, enters in through the heart chakra, radiating peace and clarity within your own heart, your own self. The Crème Soft White/Soft Yellow Rose Ray, having entered through your heart, is radiating outwards.

    Mother Mary's rose petals gently scrub each cell, each DNA fiber in your heart to a bright shine. Each rose petal exfoliates and reawakens each cell, to the very DNA, revealing Divine radiance to your self, those beloved to you, and to others. The Rosy Crème Yellow Light rests in the heart, healing, shining, radiating.

Your heart, bathed and renewed in the Rosy Crème Yellow Light, receives and radiates joy, wisdom, comfort, caring. The soft Rosy Crème Yellow Light continues to warm your heart.

Allow the Crème Soft White/Soft Yellow Rose Ray to rest in the heart area as long as needed. Mother Mary is lovingly and carefully guiding the Crème Soft White/Soft Yellow Rose Ray, radiating, emanating from the heart area.

Continue to breathe. Begin to feel Mother Mary's radiance and light all around you—you are enveloped in radiance and soft Rosy Crème Yellow Light.

In through the heart, spreading, spreading, the Crème Soft White/Soft Yellow Rose Ray continues to move, resting in the throat.

Continue to breathe. As the Rosy Crème Yellow Light rests in the throat, each rose petal is offering its cleansing and rejuvenating radiance to each eagerly awaiting cell. Your voice is intoned with comfort and empathy.

Continue to breathe. The Rosy Crème Yellow Light continues to radiate upwards, pausing, that the eyes may see with discernment and unconditional love. The Crème Soft White/Soft Yellow Rose Ray pauses, rests, clears and rejuvenates the eyes. Your vision is Divinely blessed, your perspective, Divine.

Continue to breathe, and the Crème Soft White/Soft Yellow Rose Ray moves to the ears. *How* you listen radiates love and empathy. *Listen with your spiritual body. Respond with your spiritual guidance, with the ONE within you.*

The Crème Soft White/Soft Yellow Rose Ray continues to radiate to the mind, where the thoughts are purified with gentleness and clarity, thoughtfulness and consideration, with unconditional love and comfort. Your *I AM* radiates wisdom, joy, comfort and caring. The comfort may be for your self. The comfort may be for another.

Pause, with the light of the Crème Soft White/Soft Yellow Rose Ray resting within, and radiating outwards from your eyes,

Crème Soft White/Soft Yellow Rose Ray

from your thoughts, from your listening ears. Allow the Crème Soft White/Soft Yellow Rose Ray to rest in the receiving and the offering of comfort, to self and others.

Envision Mother Mary enfolding you within her arms, as the Crème Soft White/Soft Yellow Rose Ray radiates both outwards and inwards, roses opening all around you and within you—especially in your heart chakra.

Consider the Crème Soft White/Soft Yellow Rose Ray as a breeze which comes gently by, caressing you with rose petals of empathy and vitality.

The light of this healing ray and Mother Mary permeates through your very skin—the radiance and the fragrance of the rose petals becomes part of us, reawakening our own enlightenment, reawakening our awareness of our environments—physical, mental, spiritual and emotional.

Continue the Holy Breath, beloveds, knowing Mother Mary to be holding you, surrounding you within Her love. You are safe. *I forgive and release my mental body. I forgive and release my emotional body. I forgive and release my physical body.* I allow only my spiritual body to empathize.

Continue to breathe, and to be alert, beloveds. *My compassion within my spiritual body is reawakened and enlivened. My spiritual passion is reawakened and enlivened.*

Continue the Holy Breath. The rose petals and light of the Crème Soft White/Soft Yellow Rose Ray are now also in your aura, exfoliating—almost as one receives a facial—your aura. Clear, refreshed, rejuvenated, your aura more clearly receives and expresses empathy and comfort.

Continue the Holy breath, beloveds. Perhaps you find yourself or another in a crisis situation, where discernment and empathy especially serve.

Sympathy from the emotional and mental bodies often undermines, sometimes muddles and confuses, obscuring choices and paths of action or inaction which best serve. Empathy creates the energy to offer comfort, clarity, and help to elevate self as well as others. Gain strength and power when you offer Divine empathy and thoughtfulness to yourself or another.

Empathize. Gain strength and power when offering yourself or another Spirit's unconditional love with Mother Mary's Crème Soft White/Soft Yellow Rose Ray. The Crème Soft White/Soft Yellow Rose Ray helps you to discern when to speak and when to remain silent; to pause, think, and listen; when to act and when to choose not to act. Instead of just looking at a situation or condition, you now view with a perspective of Divine empathy and comfort.

Closing Affirmation

Wisdom I AM. Comfort I AM. Radiance I AM. Joy I AM. Without effort, I AM. Joy I radiate. Comfort I radiate. Wisdom I radiate.

Closing Prayer

Mother Mary, I thank You for this healing. As I AM in this moment infused with the Rosy Crème Yellow Light, I intend to continue to Divinely discern and Divinely practice empathy instead of sympathy, to be an instrument of comfort, empathy, clarity and inspiration to myself and others. Allow me to continue to notice in every moment my Divine, vibrant connection to the ONE.

Author's note: Mother Mary and the Soft White/Soft Yellow Rose Ray arrive in warmth. Often for me, the arrival of the healing rays and Holy Masters is subtle, but not this time. I experienced very defined "butterflies" in my heart area as the meditation started, and my fingers tingled with the energy of this healing ray as the meditation progressed. As the light moved up, I enjoyed a sense of comfort, and the physical sense of "butterflies" subsided into a general warmth in my heart area. I appreciated and could relate to the image of the fragrance and presence of the rose petals accompanying the healing light. I experienced a true sense of warmth with this healing ray, and an awareness of the gentle, powerful and loving presence of Mother Mary.

Chapter Twenty-Two

Lavender Ray of Compassion and Nurturing
Lady Quan Yin, Divine Goddess of Mercy, Compassion and Charity

Love and treat yourself as you would love and treat another.
Love and treat another as you would love and treat yourself.
Melodrama is not necessary.

Opening Affirmation
Compassion and love I AM without limit.
Compassion and love I offer without limit.
Compassion and love I receive without limit.
Compassion in Action I AM.

Opening Prayer
Where my heart is locked, allow compassion be the key which opens my heart to Divine light and unconditional love. Where there are jagged, sharp edges within my heart, allow compassion to soften and smooth the gentle path, that I may offer and receive Divine energies, to be of service to myself and others. I intend to notice where my thoughts and deeds can serve to nurture myself and others to grow strong and thrive. Enfold me always in light, to live a life transforming Divine compassion into action.

Invitation and Permission

I invite Lady Quan Yin and the Lavender Ray of Compassion and nurturing into my heart, my soul, and all four bodies. I give my permission to fully allow Lady Quan Yin to direct the Lavender Ray to any part of all four bodies where it is most needed. I allow the Divine Lavender Ray to reawaken the DNA in my physical body.

Compassion, nurturing and love are inseparable. *Nurturing, the soul of compassion, is compassion in action.* Where love and nurturing are alive, compassion thrives.

Compassion is the loving view of any other expression. Nurturing is the active expression of compassion: active service with Divine love. To nurture is to take action which serves.

How do these gifts express? Compassion in action can be a healing touch, a kind thought or word of encouragement and acknowledgment, a loving smile, a laugh or two at the time when laughter is needed, a prayer, companionship. No melodrama is necessary.

Compassion and nurturing exemplify the absence of judgment, the presence, the gesture of love. You do not have to walk a mile in someone else's sandals or designer shoes, but it is necessary to envision oneself in the circumstances of another for a few steps.

In this way, as we begin to discern the experience of another, our hearts and minds open to compassion and nurturing action. Our awareness becomes acute. We *discern* what form of active service is strengthening and comforting to another, or to ourselves.

Seek your sacred space. Begin the Holy Breath. You are breathing in Spirit, and the unconditional love and mercy which are so much a part of compassion and nurturing. You are breathing in the awareness of what *action* is needed to nurture. Breathe out any negative energies through the mouth.

Lavender Ray of Compassion and Nurturing

Envision the gentlest, softest lavender color. I invite Lady Quan Yin, Divine Goddess of Mercy, Compassion and Charity, with her strength, gentility and grace, and the Lavender Ray of Compassion and Nurturing into my heart center.

Lady Quan Yin is already lovingly with you, enfolding you in her energies. The Lavender Ray begins to envelop you. Feel the palms of your hands become warm, emanating the energies of the Lavender Ray.

Your hands have become healing instruments, continuing to pulsate and warm with the energies of Lady Quan Yin and the Lavender Ray. Nurture and heal yourself (compassion in action) with the Lavender Light and energy radiating from your hands.

Breathe in the Lavender Ray. Breathe out negativity and doubt. You might consider, as you continue the Holy Breath, your intentions for action or inaction, (towards yourself, another, or a situation) which are not merciful or not energized by Divine compassion. Breathe these energies out into the Lavender Ray for transformation.

A wavy Lavender Light Mist envelops you as you continue to breathe in the Lavender Ray of Compassion and Nurturing.

Place your hands over your eyes. Feel the heat as the Lavender Ray clears your sight in order to view with compassion. Continue to nurture yourself by continuing the action of moving your hands slowly around your head.

With the Lavender energies radiating from your hands, you elevate your awareness to think and act from the compassionate and nurturing perspective, towards yourself and others.

Continue the Holy Breath. Move your hands now over your ears, and feel the heat and energies of the Lavender Ray penetrate into your ears. Listen with the inclination of compassion, and the readiness for nurturing (action).

Now move your hands to your throat, where the truth is spoken, where silence is also Divine, where words are given sound. Continue to feel the heat from your hands. The truthful, nurturing word or deed is offered in the perfect moment, in the Divine, compassionate perspective.

Move your hands over your heart. Feel the heat of the Lavender Ray continue to emanate from both of your hands into your heart. The Lavender Ray settles in your heart, strengthening it. As water might wash away layers of clogged deposits, Lady Quan Yin seeks out and lovingly dissolves the layers of hardness which have concealed the flow, glow and radiances of your heart chakra.

Continue to breathe. In the heart chakra are gentility, love, strength, courage, compassion, the will and wisdom to act or not act (nurture) as Divinely appropriate. You are enveloped in the Lavender Ray.

Hands near your heart: close your eyes and rest in the Lavender Ray. Breathe in the Lavender Light, feel misty Lavender warmth and vitality permeate your entire being, even into your pores. *Compassion I AM. Nurturer I AM. Love I AM. Mercy I AM. Patience I AM.* Continue to rest in the Lavender Ray mist as long you wish.

Open your eyes. As you begin seeing, listening and speaking, you express Divine compassion and Divine nurturing. You have the knowledge and intuition to transform compassion into action, in perfect alignment to the person (including yourself) or situation in need.

Closing Affirmation

Love I AM. Love I offer. Gentility and strength I AM. Gentility and strength I offer. Compassion in action I AM. Compassion and nurturing I offer.

Closing Prayer

Lady Quan Yin, keep me in the light, to maintain my fresh outlook of compassion in (nurturing) action; to notice the opportunity to take action, even a smile or a word of encouragement, to nurture and serve. I ask for extraordinary awareness, to notice the moment when I can offer compassion and nurturing to myself and another. Light my way to notice when I need to refresh and return to the Lavender Ray. I thank Spirit and Lady Quan Yin, Divine Goddess of Mercy, Compassion and Charity, for this healing, this reawakening of the Divine within me.

Author's note: I found the Lavender Ray of Lady Quan Yin to be very soothing and warming. I experienced a *very physical* as well as spiritual sense of being enveloped in a warm, Lavender Ray mist. The actual, physical sense of pulsating energy in my hands was encouraging and very powerful. The heat emanating from my hands, especially when held the over my heart, was strong and heartening.

Distracting moments and past events came to mind, when it seemed that if I had used the Lavender Ray, the outcomes would have likely been different. Lady Quan Yin's Lavender Ray meditation was comforting, because part of Her teaching is to have compassion for ourselves as well as others. I blessed these past experiences, resumed the Holy Breath and once again returned focus.

Chapter Twenty-Three

Amber Ray of Devotion

*For the healing of the sense of disconnect, sense of indifference.
Re-establishment of sense and awareness of connection in prayer
and communication with Spirit in every moment.*

Lady Quan Yin, Divine Goddess of Mercy, Compassion and Charity

*Your connection to and from Spirit is wide open,
cleared for take off, and so are you!*

Opening Affirmation
Devoted I AM. Holy I AM. Worthy I AM. Willing, I AM, to trust myself and Spirit. My connection to the Divine is restored and deepened.
Spirit is connected to me. I AM connected to Spirit.

Opening Prayer
I offer what trust and faith I have in this moment, and my **willingness** to trust. I intend my willingness to (re)experience a vibrant, evident connection to Spirit, to the Divine, to enjoy an abundant awareness of the Divine. I intend my soul's desire to communicate freely **to and with** Spirit, and receive Divine energies and communication *from* Spirit with clarity and assurance. I intend my prayer and my intention that every breath brings me closer to my awareness of Spirit, to my (re)connection to the ONE.

Invitation and Permission

I invite Lady Quan Yin and the Amber Ray of Devotion into my heart, my soul, and all four bodies. I give my permission to fully allow Lady Quan Yin to direct the Amber Ray to any part of all four bodies where it is most needed. I allow the Divine Amber Ray to reawaken the DNA in my physical body.

Beloveds—there are times when each of you feels alone. You are not ever alone. Spirit and your angels are always with you. Disconnection from Spirit is an illusion. When the illusion is healed, the connection is restored.

Sometimes, I hear you say: I pray, and I have the consciousness of connection in prayer. Other times I pray, and I feel as if I may just as well be talking to the wall, for all the connection or peace of I can feel.

*Whether you are aware or not, we listen to each of your prayers. The Divine **responds** to each of your prayers.*

*Perhaps you do not feel holy (enough), "good" (enough), or trusting (enough). In Divine truth and fact, **you are always all that you need**: always holy, always worthy, and trust does live within you.*

Seek your sacred space. Begin the Holy Breath. If you feel unworthiness, "unholiness", distrust, about yourself, a practical approach might be to consider only *this microsecond, this moment. In this Divine moment of connection to Spirit, Holy I AM, Worthy I AM, trusting I AM, connected We are.* Accept in this moment: all I need Spirit provides. I am connected.

Continue the Holy Breath. An abundance of moments follows, in which the true reality of your connection will become apparent to you. Continue to address this moment. *Willing I AM to trust myself and Spirit, and my connection with Spirit, and Spirit's connection with me. Let us begin the healing for the sense of disconnection, which feels so like isolation and disheartenment.*

Amber Ray of Devotion

Lady Quan Yin, I invite You and the Amber Ray of Devotion as Divine companions. Envision the deepest, most Golden honey colors as the Amber Ray of Devotion radiates around and within you in this moment. Lady Quan Yin is already with you, enfolding you in the Amber healing energies, clearing the connection, tuning up the volume of reception, to and from Spirit.

Be alert and aware, beloveds. You are Divinely connected. You are Divinely beloved unconditionally. You are heard and supported by the Divine energies.

Continue the Holy Breath. Lady Quan Yin, directing the Amber Ray, reminds your entire being in all four bodies: you are as a giant amplifier, dual purpose, ultra intense. You send and receive messages on the highest frequency. Each message *you send to Spirit is received* by Spirit. In return, *Spirit responds directly* to each of your messages, your prayers.

Continue the Holy Breath. Your perception of your connection may need to be un-muddled. Instead of the clear connection, as in glowing, open fiber optic cables, you might sense places where the fiber optics are clogged, tangled or torn—interfering with your experience of communication to and from your heavenly Friends. Think of the Amber Ray as sort of a light-driven roto rooter, clearing, intensifying, and opening up Golden communication.

Perhaps you may feel the glowing Amber warmth on your right side as the Amber Ray of Devotion expands into your heart. In the heart, the Golden Amber Light is pausing, clearing, cleansing, revitalizing each cell and DNA strand, clearing the "static," (re)opening your clear connection to receive and send messages.

We listen to the messages sent from your heart, beloveds, and in turn we send the Divine energies of Unconditional love, compassion and devotion back into your heart.

The Amber Ray loves each cell and DNA strand, resting, completing its Golden tour of your heart. The Amber Light continues to radiate throughout your being.

Continue the Holy Breath. The Amber Light is expanding, radiating as a brilliant sun or star, across your shoulders, up to your head. The Golden Amber Ray cloaks each cell in your brain, healing, soothing, smoothing the jagged darkened edges, bringing brightness and light.

The bright and clear DNA strands and cells are enhanced. The Amber Ray continues throughout the brain, seeking, healing those cells which are discouraged, their light covered over. Each cell, each DNA strand, waiting so long for light, is greeted, loved, restored to wholeness.

Continue the Holy Breath. Envision your connection being cleared with the spinning Amber light, clearing, opening, healing, brightening.

The Amber Ray continues to radiate to the spinal cord, clearing and cleansing again, reawakening all DNA. Guided by Lady Quan Yin, the Amber Ray glows down the spinal cord inch by inch, clearing, cleansing, strengthening the transmitter frequencies, sender and receiver.

Continue the Holy Breath. Beloveds, this laser Amber Ray is opening your Golden telephone line, creating a powerful, clear Golden Cord of Amber Light to and from Spirit!

The Amber Ray magnifies your being into a giant receiver, powered by light. The prayers and energies transmitted to Spirit travel up the Golden Cord created by the Amber Ray, clear and strong. In turn, you receive Divine energies, Divine *transmissions,* clear and strong.

Continue the Holy Breath. Envision your prayers, conversations, thoughts and energies as beams of light magnified by optical fibers, rocketing up the Golden connection; as powerful as the beams of light are countless.

You are a perfect vessel of Divine energy. You send and receive as the greatest transmitter in the world, contained with in you.

The healing of the Amber Ray of Devotion will take a few days or more to integrate—each moment deepens the healing.

When you sense a disconnect or feel discouraged, be still, rest, invite Lady Quan Yin and the Amber Ray of Devotion to strengthen your awareness and the flow of energy and connection with Spirit. With Lady Quan Yin, you fine tune your connection as you would tune in perfect reception on your radio.

Lady Quan Yin envelops and enfolds you in Her shimmering Light and Her radiant love, and blesses you. Divine Goddess of Mercy, Compassion and Charity, Lady Quan Yin is available to you in a thought and a moment with the Amber Ray and other rays to serve and heal you. You are a clear and perfect channel of Divine light. *You send and receive splendidly.*

Closing Affirmation
I AM a perfectly clear, Golden connection to and from Spirit. I AM a Divine transmitter, sending and receiving perfectly and clearly.

Closing Prayer
Once again, Spirit, I AM aware that my prayers are not only heard but listened to, as my connection to the Divine is restored and deepened. I intend to notice the many fun and miraculous ways in which my prayers are answered. As I see Golden Amber colors each day, I intend to be reminded of our loving Lady Quan Yin, the vibrant Amber Ray and my clear, deep connection to the Divine. I offer my thanks to the Divine and my intention to keep the connection, with Amber energies, recharged, tuned in, clear and perfect.

Author's note: The energies of Lady Quan Yin seemed to begin with a sense of radiance and warmth, almost butterflies, in my heart area, and more subtly, on my right side. The energies seemed to radiate, to expand out from my heart, across my shoulders, arms and fingertips, up to the top of my head, radiating along my back. I enjoyed this radiating warmth both as a healing and a confirmation of being enveloped by Archangel Uriel's Divine energies.

Chapter Twenty-Four

Navy Blue Ray for the Elevation of Spirit
Archangel Uriel,
Archangel of Transformation

*For the healing of the spirit.
Let our souls be uplifted, that we may have
constant and immediate access to the Divine, in all
matters, in all forms, in all moments.
We are not asked, in this moment, to trust.
We are only asked to be daring,
to be willing to trust.*

Opening Affirmation
Daring, I AM. Willing to trust, I AM. My soul is uplifted, my conscious access to the Divine immediate, clear and perfect.

Opening Prayer
I offer this prayer to Spirit, to Archangel Uriel. Uplift my soul, my spirit, that I may know instant, clear access to the Divine. Reignite my sense of daring that I may dare to trust my perfect connection to the Divine, in the deepest and highest levels. Though I may not feel especially strong or connected to my self or my faith at this moment, I invite Archangel Uriel into my very being, to enfold me and hold me during this healing, and guide the Navy Blue Ray. I proclaim my intention that I will emerge from this healing with my spirit whole, healed, radiant and

stronger than ever, elevated to commune with and access Divine energy in any and all moments.

Invitation and Permission
I invite Archangel Uriel and the Navy Blue Ray for the Elevation of Spirit into my heart, my soul, and all four bodies. I give my permission to fully allow Archangel Uriel to direct the Navy Blue Light to any part of all four bodies where it is most needed. I allow the Navy Blue Light to reawaken the DNA in my physical body.

Sometimes, Spirit waits to hear even this question: *Can I trust? Dare I be willing to trust?* Spirit reignites your sense of daring, your willingness to trust. The sense of separation, distance, isolation from the Divine is diminished and healed. Perceived lack of connection is transformed to clear, immediate, perfectly tuned-in access.

Jagged piercing by worldly energies of our spiritual, emotional, and mental bodies results in injury to those bodies, as much in need of healing as any injury to the physical body.

As a physical body is battered and wounded, so our personal spirit and soul is wounded. For this reason we must be vigilant guardians of our soul's robust health.

The soul wounds leak energy, the same as a physical injury might leak life's blood. As a physician mends a bleeding wound in the physical body, Archangel Uriel and the Navy Blue Ray for the Elevation of Spirit heal a wounded spirit. Be daring to heal.

Once again, know and accept that you are worthy to receive Divine healing rays and Divine intervention. The perceived sense separation and disconnect from Spirit is an illusion, and is unnecessary.

Navy Blue Ray for the Elevation of Spirit

Worthy I Am. Holy I Am. Give voice to this affirmation, beloveds. Express yourself grandly, loudly. *Worthy I AM to receive Divine Healing. Holy I AM. Whole I AM.*

Seek your sacred space. Begin the Holy Breath. If you become distracted, begin again and count the breaths. Archangel Uriel, I invite you and the Divine Navy Blue Ray for the Healing and Elevation of Spirit.

I, Archangel Uriel, Archangel of Transformation, hold you. I enfold you, in this moment and any moment in which you call me forth.

Archangel Uriel wants you to know: *Worthy you are, whether you feel like it or not. At one with Spirit you are, whether you feel like it, perceive it or not. When you are wounded in spirit, it is most difficult to accept that you are worthy, to trust your access to the Divine. I indeed see your precious Divinity, and know that you are worthy of Divine healing. How could it be otherwise? You are a spark of God, a Divine part of the ONE.*

Archangel Uriel again encourages and informs you: *I stand with you. I enfold you within my most holy and powerful wings. I prepare, with the power of the Navy Blue Ray, to heal and elevate your Spirit, so precious, so Divinely beloved. Your Spirit has been longing for this moment of healing and transformation.*

Continue the holy Breath. Say out loud: *Daring I AM. Worthy I AM. Holy I AM. Ready I AM to receive a Divine healing.* Use a stronger voice: *Daring I AM. Worthy I AM. Whole I AM. Ready I AM to receive and manifest Divine healing in this and all moments.*

Continue to breathe. Open and receive the Divine courage and comfort which are being offered to you.

Do not think that you have to "tough it out". Rest, relax, trust. Allow at this time the Navy Blue Ray, with Archangel Uriel's guidance, to transform and heal.

Continue the Holy Breath. Envision the Navy Blue Ray, a deep, dark, rich blue, radiant, shimmering in its depth. Rest. Envision yourself enfolded within this radiant, Navy Blue Light. The Navy Blue is Divinely radiant rather than dark. You are safe and protected.

Guided by Archangel Uriel, the Navy Blue Ray arrives on your upper right side, behind and slightly above you, and radiates towards your head. Radiant, the deep Navy Blue Light pauses in the brain, moving gently into the spinal cord, and central nervous system.

Your head, your throat, shoulder, arms are infused with the Navy Blue light. Feel the lightness. Feel the expansion. Feel your fingertips tingle.

Continue to breathe. Archangel Uriel continues illuminate, to seek, to heal, carefully diagnosing your spirit, transforming and healing with the Navy Light the injuries, the erroneous perceptions of separation from Spirit, into radiant strength and health. The Navy Blue Ray for the Elevation of Spirit may pause longer in some areas than in others, guided by Archangel Uriel.

Your healing is complete, and continues to integrate over a period of several days.

Archangel Uriel invites you to use this healing at any moment when you begin to perceive a sense of separation or distance from Spirit, to elevate your spirit and restore your own constant, immediate, and holy access to the ONE, your sense of self as part of the ONE.

Archangel Uriel leaves his gifts with you: his loving energies and the energies of the Navy Blue Ray, strengthening you with every breath.

Closing Affirmation
I express myself Divinely.
I AM an expression of the Divine.
My Spirit is raised, transformed, strong and whole.
Connected to God, constantly, without separation, a part of the ONE, I AM.

Closing Prayer
From heart and soul, I offer this prayer of gratitude. Entering this meditation wounded in spirit, I emerge transformed, spirit raised and healed. Immediate access to the Divine energies, to the ONE, is recharged, restored. I intend to recognize the wounds to my spirit that I may notice and be aware to call upon Archangel Uriel in my moment of need. I am grateful to continue to be enfolded in the wings of the Archangel of Transformation and to enjoy the healing energies of the radiant Navy Blue Ray, as they integrate within me.

Author's note: My experience was that the Navy Blue Ray seemed to enter through my right side, and radiate very quickly outwards to my head, across my shoulders, down my back, to my heart area—almost all at the same time. I was very aware of my heartbeat, and as the Navy Blue Ray flowed down my arms, I felt almost a slight electrical charge in my fingertips. As the healing progressed, I had a strong sense of the Navy Blue Ray and the energies of Archangel Uriel expanding throughout my entire being, until I felt completely filled with Archangel Uriel's energies, inside and outside.

Chapter Twenty-Five

Aqua Ray: Exaltation and Glory in Spirit, Exaltation and Glory of Spirit
Archangel Uriel,
Archangel of Transformation

We are One with Spirit .
Rejoice in Spirit Indwelling.
Kinsmanship!

Opening Affirmation
I notice Divine glory and beauty around me
in all circumstances.
I AM Divinely glorious and I AM Divine beauty,
in all circumstances.

Opening Prayer
Precious Spirit, I intend to notice that any moment is the best moment to simply enjoy myself in Spirit, in my connection as part of the One. As I exalt, glorify, and delight in Spirit, I also exalt, glorify and delight in my soul and person, the being who I AM. For my connection, as part of the ONE, as a spark of God, I thank You. I invite Archangel Uriel, Archangel of Transformation, and the Aqua Ray to uplift my spirit and celebrate the ONE in all moments, in all ways.

Invitation and Permission

I invite Archangel Uriel and the Aqua Ray for the Exaltation and Glory in Spirit and of Spirit into my heart, my soul, and all four bodies. I give my permission to fully allow Archangel Uriel to direct the Aqua Light to any part of all four bodies where it is most needed. I allow the Aqua Light to reawaken the DNA in my physical body.

Sometimes we simply need to enjoy! To exalt in Spirit is also to exalt in who we are in Spirit.

Let us rejoice. Rejoice that we are part of the One. As we praise and love Spirit, we praise and love our Divine selves. Consider your thoughts, deeds and actions as praise of Spirit and self. Exalt in Spirit, and exalt in self.

Envision the Aqua Ray: liquid brilliance, not quite turquoise and not quite green or blue, shimmering, radiant.

Seek your sacred space. Begin the Holy Breath. I invite and I welcome Archangel Uriel and the Aqua Ray for the Exaltation and Glory *of* Spirit and *in* Spirit.

Continue the Holly Breath. The Aqua Ray enters from the right side of your head, almost at the top. Feel your fingertips tingle as the Aqua Ray begins its joyous journey.

In a glorious, breathtaking family reunion, the Aqua Ray and Archangel Uriel greet and recognize each molecule, each cell, each DNA strand, as a precious, delightful, and *familiar* part of Spirit, of God.

Continue the Holy Breath. The Aqua Ray and Archangel Uriel greet your DNA. Igniting or re-igniting takes place and the realization and recollection occurs: God I AM! Part of the ONE I AM! Huzzah! Let's celebrate this good news!

The Aqua Ray may encounter some DNA strands which have forgotten their connection. The Aqua Light, liquid and brilliant, lovingly bathes each cell which has forgotten, reminding, *transforming,* reconnecting. Part of the ONE you are!

As the Aqua Ray greets, reunites and transforms, consider your kinsmanship. You are kin to the Universe, and the Universe is kin to you. You are connected, related, relating, part of one another. Notice your environment, and the way you fit into your surroundings.

As you are part of Spirit, part of ONE, everything alive on the planet is also part of Spirit. In this way, you are profoundly connected to one another, and to Spirit.

Continue the Holy Breath. The Aqua ray reminds your eyes. Rejoice, the sights which you behold. Holiness is in all life! Be glad of your Divine perspective and vision, and the vision you present to others; not only the way you look, but also the energies which you emanate.

Continue the Holy Breath. The Aqua Ray continues to flow. In your ears, the Aqua light bathes each cell, each nerve. Rejoice, the sounds you hear. Are there birds, music? Glorious are the sounds, in turn, you create in joy and praise. *Be selective*, and be glad of what you hear when you listen.

Continue the Holy Breath. The Aqua Ray Light, fluid, bathes your mouth, your throat, pausing to transform the dormant cells, to reignite those which have forgotten that they are indeed a part of the Universe, of God. Sing out loud! Hear your voice resonate and connect with the sounds of the Universe!

The Aqua Ray continues the joyous journey, now into the heart. It is in the heart where the Aqua Light—liquid, brilliant, shimmering Aqua, rests.

Rejoice! Exalt in your connection of your own heart with the heart of Spirit! The Aqua Light, greeting each awake DNA strand, is also transforming sleepy, forgetful DNA in your heart, reminding your heart of your own connection to the ONE. Continue the Holy Breath. As you exalt in God, exalt in yourself!

Archangel Uriel continues to guide the Aqua Ray in the joy-full journey, greeting, reuniting your DNA strands which remember their connection to the ONE, transforming and reminding those which have forgotten.

Fluid and shimmering, the Aqua Light radiates, greeting and reminding, enjoying your exaltation in self and Spirit.

Hands and feet, voice and movement, song and dance, with thought and action: glorify, *celebrate Spirit and self.* Enjoy!

Notice the Divine harmony which you behold in all things. In turn, notice the Divine harmony which you present to all others around you. Exalt in your kinsmanship to each aspect of life—the song of the bird, the fragrance of flowers, the air, sun, the wetness of rain, the weather; everything is a part of you and you are a part of everything.

Each breath, each thought is a miracle. Continue to exalt with the Aqua Ray.

Closing Affirmation
Connected to God, I AM. Kin to the Universe, and all life, I AM.
As I exalt in God, I exalt in God within me.

Closing Prayer
As I enjoy and celebrate Spirit and myself as a part of Spirit, I intend to notice my kinsmanship to all life and to the Universe. Gift me with the Divine perspective to love, care and respect myself as I love and respect God. Keep me alert to care for my kin—all life—on this planet, with the same love, compassion and respect, with which I Divinely care for myself.

Author's note: I could feel the warmth of the Aqua Ray, very lovingly on my right side, from behind me. I also felt lightness and a pulsating, or tingling, in my fingertips, as the Aqua Ray seemed to radiate towards my head, expand across my shoulders, down my arms, to my fingertips. I was aware, simultaneously, of a sense of excitement in my heart area, of Aqua energies radiating in my head, and the sense of the Aqua energies glowing within and around my entire upper body. I truly experienced a sense of lightness, of elevation, of being very large, a sense of being raised and uplifted as the energies celebrated Spirit I AM. The excitement in the heart area remained throughout the meditation.

Chapter Twenty-Six

Red Ray of Courage

Integrating the energies of Courage, Faith, Truth, and Hope (Divine confidence)

Archangel Uriel, Archangel of Transformation

To help summon and recognize already inward dwelling faith and courage.

Often used in partnership with St. Germaine and the Violet Flame of Transmutation
and/or
Archangel Michael and the Chartreuse Ray to Go Deeper into Discernment

Opening Affirmation
I have and ***I AM*** *all the faith, truth and hope I need, in any moment.*
I have and ***I AM*** *all the courage which I need, in any moment.*
I AM surrounded by Divine, invincible protection.

Opening Prayer
Archangel Uriel, I invite you and the Red Ray of Courage to reawaken and restore the energies of courage within me, to reawaken my very DNA. I intend to discern the path and direction which is blessed, to know and recognize my own faith and courage. I intend to discern the presence my personal Celestial

Army of the Invincible Divine, to be aware to call upon You, Archangel Uriel, and the Divine Red Ray, to reawaken my faith, hope and courage, in this and any moment. Guide and protect my steps, precious Spirit, that I may only take the best and highest course of action in my mental, emotional, physical and spiritual bodies.

Invitation and Permission
I invite Archangel Uriel and the Red Ray of Courage into my heart, my soul, and all four bodies. I give my permission to fully allow Archangel Uriel to direct the Red Light to any part of all four bodies where it is most needed. I allow the Red Light to reawaken the DNA in my physical body.

While we focus on *courage,* the energies of faith, truth, hope and courage are not individual or separate from each other. Faith, truth, hope and courage are integrated energies. When one energy expresses, all express to varying degrees.

We are all *already courageous.* Sometimes we don't feel or recognize the courage we have within ourselves.

At times, some of the courage has been clouded or hidden by fear. Archangel Uriel brings us the Red Ray of Courage, transforming the fear, (re)activating the very DNA of our courage, bringing our courage forward in limitless abundance.

Do you remember learning to ride a bicycle, or play an instrument? Practice transformed an activity which seemed difficult (or impossible) into a routine, which you could summon with a thought or action.

Such can be your experience with courage. Invite Archangel Uriel and the Red Ray of Courage with a breath, an invitation, a prayer, at any moment, in any situation, to (re)activate your courage, to *transform* fear into courage. Archangel Uriel is listening, waiting, for your invitation.

Courage is an excellent habit. Archangel Uriel asks your awareness, beloveds: *while fear is a form of habit, courage can also become a habit. Choose!*

First, in this meditation do not be afraid of "not getting it." You are already "getting it," being successful, simply by getting this far in the healing. The victory, the blessing, your abundant courage, is already demonstrated and proven, simply by this endeavor.

Seek your sacred space. Begin your Holy Breath. If you are out and about, and need Archangel Uriel and the Red Ray of Courage, create your sacred space with the Holy Breath.

At this moment, in your sacred space, know that you deserve Divine healing and attention. In fact, in any and all moments, a Divine laser of love is focused upon you.

I invite Archangel Uriel and the Divine Red Ray of Courage. I know that within this Divine Red Ray of Courage, the energies of faith, hope and discernment of the truth are also integrated, being brought forth for me as well.

Envision a deep red: brilliant, shimmering and vibrant. Not with orange tones, but vividly deep red, almost with a lavender flashing of light, as in a brilliant ruby. All facets glisten.

You are enfolded in the powerful and loving wings of Archangel Uriel. You are safe.

Continue to breathe. *I AM encompassed by this Red Ray of Courage, by Archangel Uriel. I AM, in fact, covered and protected in Red Light, in courage, as a knight might be covered in a suit of armor.*

Within this Red Ray you are infused with courage, ability, willingness, the very faith to act. You are safe, protected, no harm can come to you.

Continue the Holy Breath. The Divine is all powerful, invincible! No power (situation, condition) is greater than Divine Light. You are a Divine aspect of the Divine ONE!

Keep in mind who you have in your corner—Spirit, Archangel Uriel enfolding you in His wings, the Divine Red Ray of Courage, your own angels, your own Divine self. A formidable Celestial Army!

Never underestimate Divine protection. Your personal Celestial Army is here, responding instantly to your invitation to Divinely transform fear into courage. Remember, Archangel Uriel is *transforming* fears into courage.

Continue the Holy Breath. Archangel Uriel's mission is twofold. First, to help you deal with individual fears, getting more and more into practice, until the Red Ray of Courage becomes routine and automatic. Also, to unmask, reawaken, reactivate your cells and DNA strands of courage which have been dormant, covered over for the moment by fear, restoring your courageous vibrancy already indwelling.

Continue the Holy Breath. Envision the Red Ray of Courage, infusing you, strengthening you.

Perhaps there may be small fears nagging and stealing upon you, like a fog, limiting your vision and your ability to act, for fear of what may lay ahead.

Summon a fear which you are holding at this moment for transformation.

Let's start with smaller, more manageable fears. Use the Red Ray of Courage to help you confront or summon the fear in all of its aspects.

As we become strengthened in the Divine Red Ray of Courage, we continue to move forward with other, greater fears.

The Red Ray of Courage enters from the right side of the body, spreading warmth where the chill of fear has made a *temporary* home.

Archangel Uriel and the Red Ray of Courage are not here to instill courage you may (erroneously) perceive to be lacking. Rather, Archangel Uriel and the Red Ray of Courage **reawaken and resurrect the courage which you already have within you, indwelling in your heart and soul!**

Down through your head the Red Light radiates, resting, healing each area, reawakening, resurrecting, transforming each cell, each DNA fiber which fear has covered and made asleep.

Recognize that you are huge and courageous with the Red Ray and your angels protecting you. Your Celestial Army is with you, a part of you now and always, simply for the invitation. You and your reawakened courage are bigger than the fear, as the ocean is bigger than a puddle in the street. The fear diminishes, snapping into focus and perspective.

Continue to breathe. The Red Ray of Courage continues to radiate in your head and in your heart, searing hot, transforming each cell, each molecule, each DNA strand which has known fear, releasing, healing, refreshing, transforming, restoring.

The Red Ray has empowered you to be stronger than that which you fear, to recognize the invincibility of the Divine ONE of which you are such an important aspect.

Continue the Holy Breath. The Red Ray, with Archangel Uriel's direction, seeks each cell, each DNA strand in each part of your body, where fear often resides, transforming, glowing, resting in each organ.

Continue the Holy Breath, feel the warmth of the Red Ray move down your body to your solar plexus, your legs, to the soles of your feet. The Red Ray continues as a diffused laser light, seeking, healing, transforming, resurrecting.

The Red Ray surrounds you, infuses you, diffuses throughout you, filling you with the knowledge of your own truth—*I AM ONE with the INVINCIBLE power of Spirit, my angels, the Holy Masters.* The fear is broken, transformed. Its power over you is no more.

I AM worthy. I AM holy. I AM deserving of Divine intervention. I AM heard and listened to. My own courage reawakened, I AM strong and courageous in my own self and in Spirit.

The Red Ray of Courage can be used in partnership with *St. Germaine and the Violet Flame of Transmutation and Archangel Michael and the Chartreuse Ray to go Deeper into Discernment.* Call forth and invite as you feel appropriate.

Closing Affirmation
Divinely courageous, Divinely daring, I AM, without limit.
Divinely aware of and ready to call upon my
Celestial Army, I AM.

Closing Prayer
Thank you, Archangel Uriel, for the Divine journey of healing. I accept my courage, I accept my daring, I accept my Divine Celestial Army. Thank you for this healing and transformation of fear into courage. I intend that I AM fully present with my own courage. I AM grateful to Spirit and Archangel Uriel for these gifts, for Their readiness to be with me at any moment. I AM grateful that the Red Ray of Courage only a thought and an invitation away, and I intend to use invite the Red Ray energies in any moment of desire or need.

Author's note: The energies of Archangel Uriel seem to come in from the back right side of my head. The energies of the Red Ray of Courage moved quickly to my heart, where once again, I had an acute sense of my heartbeat.

Chapter Twenty-Seven

Light Green Ray of Peace and Protection
Archangel Uriel,
Archangel of Transformation

Resolution of conflict.
Diminishing and transmutation of anger.
Gentleness and compassion.
Discover the seeds of Divine resolution
in every conflict.
What goes around comes around!

Opening Affirmation
Peace I AM. Safe and secure, Divinely protected in this and all moments, I AM. Compassionate and strong, I AM. Forgiven and Forgiving, I AM.

Opening Prayer
In this world and in this life which sometime seem so fragmented, filled with chaos and conflict, I ask for Divine peace and Divine protection from the negative energies which surround me, and that my heart and my soul be protected from injury. I ask Archangel Uriel, with His Divine guidance and love, not only to Divinely protect me, but also to transform and heal those injuries already present within me with the Light Green Ray of Peace and Protection.

Invitation and Permission

I invite Archangel Uriel and the Light Green Ray of Peace and Protection into my heart, my soul, and all four bodies. I give my permission to fully allow Archangel Uriel to direct the Light Green Ray to any part of all four bodies where it is most needed. I allow the Light Green Ray to reawaken the DNA in my physical body.

When we sometimes find ourselves in deep, dangerous water, the Light Green Ray is our lifeboat and Archangel Uriel our navigator. Let us begin with the energies of peace and protection, and move on to the resolution of conflict.

Peace I AM. My peace I give unto you. Holy I AM. Holy WE ARE. We share Divinity, the holiness, the Divine peace and protection of the ONE.

Your question: How can I find peace and protection when I feel surrounded, unnerved, by uncertainty and conflict, both internal and external? Your answer: *Find peace and protection Divinely.* Archangel Uriel and the Light Green Ray of Peace and Protection are ready to serve, awaiting your invitation.

The purpose of the Light Green Ray is to encompass, surround, and infuse you with the *Divine Light Green Shield of Peace and Protection.* Archangel Uriel and the Light Green energies create a shield both internal and external, protecting and offering peace to the mental, emotional, and spiritual bodies, as well as the physical. *The protection is the deepened alignment with the Divine—a spiritual recharge.*

By creating a shield of Light Green Light around and within you, Archangel Uriel transforms energies which do not serve you. The Light Green Light reawakens your DNA in your physical being, to remember, practice, and manifest Divine peace and protection.

Light Green Ray of Peace and Protection

Find your sacred space, and begin the Holy Breath. *Archangel Uriel, I invite you and the Light Green Ray of Peace and Protection.*

Envision the colors and energies of the Light Green Ray. What is the color of new leaves as they emerge from a branch? Not brilliant chartreuse, but soft, light green.

Continue the Holy Breath. If you lose focus, just begin again. Counting your breaths will help you focus.

Breathe in the sparkling Light Green Light. Breathe in the peace and protection energies of Archangel Uriel.

As you continue the Holy Breath, you also breathe in many bonus healing energies: courtesy and compassion, light, benevolence, purity, beneficence, angelic cloaking. Remember, beloved—purity is simply the clarity of your connection to the ONE.

Continue to breathe. The Light Green Ray enters along your right side, expanding to the head and heart, enfolding, embracing, loving, regenerating, *transforming, healing* each cell, each DNA strand which is holding any conflict or anger, or any energy which is not serving you.

Your DNA has been longing for a release, longing for the light, longing for the transformation to freedom which will finally allow peace and the awareness of Divine protection.

As the Light Green Ray expands, the shimmering light continues to locate and heal your internal and external conflicts.

Continue the Holy Breath. External conflicts are healed with the recollection, reawakening of your physical DNA by the Light Green Ray, of your Divine self, your Divine perspective. The conflicts, in Divine perspective, become manageable. Divinely inspired resolutions are revealed, allowed, inspired.

Continue the Holy Breath. Notice the Light Green Ray expanding throughout your body, healing, transforming, reawakening each cell and DNA strand, offering Divine Love and

Divine forgiveness for self and others. Divine peace is being restored, Divine protection is being provided.

Continue to breathe. The Light Green Ray surrounds the heart with the shimmering Light Green energies of Peace and Protection.

The heart is one of the places in which we hold anger, negativity, injury and fear of injury, to the detriment of all four bodies—physical, mental, emotional, spiritual. Archangel Uriel pauses in the heart, especially, clearing, cleansing, transforming, creating a shield of Light Green Ray energies, of Divine protection against injurious reactions in any of the four bodies to anger, negativity, conflict, fear.

In the heart, the Light Green Ray acts as radar, as a laser. Searching each cell, each molecule, each DNA, seeking any energies of anxiety, worries, self loathing, anger, conflict; any energies which are harmful. Each molecule in the heart is embraced with love, each DNA strand transformed, protected with the Light Green Ray of Peace and Protection.

Peace I AM. Peace I give unto you. Peace I give unto myself. Forgiveness I AM. Forgiveness I give unto you. Forgiveness I give unto myself.

Continue the Holy Breath. The Light Green Ray continues the holy mission of transformation, continuing to expand in the upper body, seeking, especially in the internal organs, those areas where any negative energy is held. Each DNA strand is transformed and healed, encompassed with a Light Green Shield, the protective Light Green Ray of Peace and Protection.

Continue the Holy Breath. Peace you are. Fully protected with the Light Green Ray, you are.

Even as the Light Green Ray of Peace and Protection creates a Divine Shield of Peace and Protection in your aura, the Light Green ray is also, with your permission, transforming your DNA to recall, to manifest Divine Peace and Protection.

Light Green Ray of Peace and Protection

Continue to breathe. Let us turn our attention to the transformation and resolution of conflict, clearly necessary to allow peace. In considering forgiveness, and holding conflict, the human response is often, *"I (really) have been wronged. My (anger) position is justified!"*

Fully acknowledge the truth and magnitude of your experience, as does Spirit. You may have been treated unfairly, betrayed. You may be indeed be "in the right". Still, beloveds, in order to allow peace, the anger must be released; the conflict must be resolved, not to serve another, <u>but to serve yourself.</u> Conflict held is harmful to all four of your bodies. <u>Move on!</u>

Continue to breathe in the Light Green Ray as Archangel Uriel continues to bless, heal and transform all energies into peace and protection.

Do you see, beloveds? Let us say you are walking along the street, and someone robs you. Enraged, you think: *Unfair! How could this person do this to me?* As your rage continues to simmer and boil, the single act has now multiplied in your heart.

While your robber has disappeared, and most probably forgotten you, you continue to be pummeled in all four bodies by the robber, blow after blow, each more harmful than the last, as you hold your anger and your fear. Energies which are not Divine are in your way.

Your responsibility is not to compel yourself to forgive or make yourself less angry. Your responsibility is only to invite, to allow the light of Divine Spirit to transform the anger, the conflict.

Saint Germaine's Violet Flame is placed before you in a breath and an invitation, and may be useful to you now.

Continue the Holy Breath. As the Light Green Ray radiates, Divine perspective is reignited. With Divine perspective, you are able to manage your situation using Divine discernment, Divine creativity, Divine forgiveness.

The Light Green Ray of Peace and Protection continues to be guided by Archangel Uriel. In every conflict, the Divine seeds of resolution are available.

Archangel Uriel and the Light Green Ray seek, discover and reveal to you the Divine seeds of resolution. With this elevated awareness, go forward and break free of the weighty and negative energies of conflict, which infringe so heavily on your own Divine peace. Love and compassion nurture the seeds of Divine resolution: the more love and compassion is offered, the more the conflict dissolves.

Call upon Archangel Uriel and the Light Green Ray of Peace and Protection in any moment of need, in any place, with a breath and an invitation. Archangel Uriel is listening for your call.

Closing Affirmation
At peace, safe and secure, I AM.
Divinely protected, within and without, I AM.
Transformed and peaceful, I AM.

Closing Prayer
For the radiant, Divine, Light Green Ray and Shield of Peace and Protection, within and without, I AM grateful. Thank you for replacing my tempestuous stormy seas with mirror calm waters. Love and compassion live within me, in all four bodies, where conflict and anger once resided. My prayer and my intention is to continue to envision and recognize the powerful Light Green Ray, the Divine Shield of Peace and Protection which I now enjoy. At anytime I feel the Light Green Shield Of Peace And Protection needs a Divine recharge, I intend to call upon You, Archangel Uriel, and Spirit, with a breath, and an invitation. I know You will once again enfold and strengthen me in the Light Green Ray of Peace and Protection.

Author's note: I experienced the warmth and sensation of Archangel Uriel's energies as arriving with a powerful sense of expansion and a strong sense of lightness, almost lift, on my right side, from behind, at the beginning of the meditation.

    Instead of moving up or down, the energies, in my experience, expanded across the shoulders, arms and fingertips, to the head, heart and solar plexus area. This sense of expansion was accompanied by the experience of being lifted, of being elevated. Once again, I was very conscious of my heart beating during the meditation.

Chapter Twenty-Eight

Dark Pink Ray for the Healing of Depression
Archangel Zoriel, Messenger of God

Depression is unnecessary.
Be uplifted: the healing is at hand.

Opening Affirmation
Beloved I AM. Divinely energetic, Divinely resilient I AM.

Opening Prayer
Spirit, I come to you feeling broken and weary: physically, mentally, emotionally and spiritually. My prayer is to be released from this state of depression, to be reawakened to the glorious and worthy person I AM in all four bodies. I request not only the healing of depression, I ask also for resilience, for the God within me to express joyfully, vibrantly, with Divine energy and awareness of who I AM in the Divine. Archangel Zoriel, Messenger of God, I invite You and the Dark Pink Ray for the Healing of Depression, aware that all the faith and trust I have in this moment is all that I need. Liberate me from depression and restore Divine awareness and vitality within me.

Invitation and Permission
I invite Archangel Zoriel and the Dark Pink Ray for Healing of Depression into my heart, my soul, and all four bodies. I give my permission to fully allow Archangel Zoriel to direct the Dark Pink Light to any part of all four bodies where it is most needed.

I allow the Dark Pink Light to reawaken the DNA in my physical body.

Depression and anxiety go hand in hand—one often causes the other. The Dark Pink Ray is for healing both the depression which anxiety brings, and the anxiety which depression brings. The personal sense of unworthiness also creates depression. Does this sound a familiar experience, beloveds?

The healing with Archangel Zoriel, Messenger of God, brings an end to the unhappy depression-anxiety-depression cycle, and sense of unworthiness. Depression and the sense of unworthiness interfere with our moving forward and being fully present with our own ONE-NESS with Spirit.

*Archangel Zoriel and the Dark Pink Ray heal depression, deeply interconnected in **all four bodies: physical, mental, emotional and spiritual. As one body is healed, so all bodies are healed.***

It is in the battering, bruising and wounding of the mental, emotional and spiritual bodies where the seeds of depression take root, grow and manifest in the physical body. Archangel Zoriel's Dark Pink Light seeks and heals each seed, each root, in each body.

Seek your sacred space. Begin the Holy Breath. Do not wait for or be anxious about the perfect time, perfect sacred space, your perfect appearance or perfect state of mind. *Your intention* makes any space and any moment perfect.

Be aware and repeat: I AM worthy. Worthy I AM. I AM holy. Holy I AM. In this moment, Archangel Zoriel stands near you, awaiting your invitation. Let us begin the meditation.

Archangel Zoriel, Messenger of God, I invite You and the Dark Pink Ray for the Healing of Depression.

Continue the Holy Breath. For the healing of depression, we seek the deepest, darkest pink—perhaps the deep pink we might find on a dark pink, almost purple rose.

Dark Pink Ray for the Healing of Depression

Archangel Zoriel, delighted, stands next to you and enfolds you. You do not need, we remind you, to earn an Archangel's or Spirit's love. It is already, unconditionally, yours.

Continue the Holy Breath. *Worthy I AM. Holy I AM. Connected to Spirit and the ONE I AM. Vitality I AM. Beloved I AM.*

You are safe and enfolded in Archangel Zoriel's wings. He has been waiting for your invitation. Your sense of unworthiness is an illusion.

The Deep Pink Ray enters from your upper back, warm, diffusing, penetrating immediately to the heart area. Radiating across your shoulders, down your arms, to the palms of your hands and fingertips, the Deep Pink light expands to your head area.

Continue the Holy Breath. The Dark Pink Ray seeks immediately those cells and DNA strands which are exhausted, inert, immobilized, and dormant. Heavy in their sleep, these cells and DNA strands have given up, contributing to the state of depression.

Continue to breathe. Messenger of God, Archangel Zoriel shines the intense Dark Pink Light upon each cell, each DNA strand, with the ultimate message from Spirit.

Wake up! You are Divinely loved! You are Divinely nurtured with unconditional love and compassion. You are not judged. Rather, you are Divinely, unconditionally loved and beloved. You are worthy!

Some of the cells and DNA strands stir with the wake up call, rising into the Dark Pink Light for the healing of Divine vitality. The Dark Pink Ray infuses each DNA strand with the Dark Pink Light of energy, healing, strength.

Other cells and DNA strands are resistant, accustomed to their lethargy. Here, Archangel Zoriel shouts the messages of God, infusing, once more, intense Dark Pink Light. Healing is taking place.

Continue to breathe. Archangel Zoriel continues the process in the heart, healing, restoring, each cell, each DNA strand, to vibrant liveliness. Your heart is restored to vitality, energy, clarity.

The Dark Pink Ray for the Healing of Depression continues to expand, meticulously, lovingly, continuing to the solar plexus, healing, awakening, revitalizing each cell, each DNA strand, each internal organ, radiating, embracing the body, head to toe.

Archangel Zoriel and the Dark Pink Ray expand the Divine Dark Pink Light, to the top of the head, the ears, the eyes, to the brain, restoring, gently whispering or shouting out loud the Divine news as needed, infusing the intense light of the Dark Pink Ray.

Continue the Holy Breath. The Dark Pink Ray, under the guidance of Archangel Zoriel, heals the brain. Once again, dormant, inert cells and DNA strands are sought out, and reawakened with the Divine unconditional love and compassion of both the Dark Pink Ray and Archangel Zoriel.

Allow the Dark Pink healing light to rest and work in the brain as long as needed. Each part of your brain, now, is loved, healed, bathed in light, restored to vitality.

Continue the Holy Breath. Accept and be thankful for the healing and holy work of Archangel Zoriel and the Dark Pink Ray for the Healing of Depression.

Don't wait to be overtaken by depression in order to call Archangel Zoriel. At the first hint of blues down to your shoes, call on Archangel Zoriel in any moment. He awaits your invitation!

Closing Affirmation

Free from paralysis I AM, in all four bodies. I AM Divinely, buoyantly energetic in my physical, mental, emotional and spiritual bodies. I AM Divinely loved. I AM Divinely glorious. I know my Divine worthiness.

Closing Prayer

Spirit, I am aware that I have only to ask for Divine intervention in all aspects of my life, and to notice the miracles offered to me. I accept my Divine worthiness, and I accept and thank Spirit for this healing for depression. Spirit, I intend to be acutely aware of my resilience, my Divine worthiness. I intend any slings and arrows shot my way can not penetrate and are deflected by my Divine Shield. I call upon Archangel Zoriel in any moment of depression, disheartenment, and discouragement, to be uplifted into the Divine Zone, to be freed from the illusion of unworthiness.

Author's note: I could feel the warmth of the healing ray in my upper back and shoulders, and especially as Archangel Zoriel directed the Dark Pink Ray to the heart, I could feel a sense of flutters or butterflies. I also could feel my hands and fingers pulsate with a general feeling of expansion.

Chapter Twenty-Nine

Flame Orange Ray
Healing of Indignity, Shame and Burning Humiliation
Archangel Jophiel,
Archangel of Illumination

Divinely love yourself, that you may
Divinely love others.
Divinely forgive yourself, that you may
Divinely forgive others.

Opening Affirmation
Dignity I AM. Grace I AM. Whole I AM.
Forgiveness I AM. Compassion I AM.
Divine love for my self, I AM.
Divine love for others, I AM.

Opening Prayer
I invite Archangel Jophiel, Archangel of Illumination, and the Flame Orange Ray for the Healing of Indignity, Shame and Burning Humiliation as my Divine partners in this holy journey. I invite the holiest of all energies to enfold me in unconditional love and compassion. As I AM beloved by You, Spirit, reveal to me, in my own heart, my own Divine love for myself and others. Open my heart to Divine compassion and forgiveness, for myself and others. As I radiate worthiness and value in Your eyes, I ask for Your Divine energies to help me discover and accept my own glorious value and worthiness, and to notice these Divine energies in others as well. I intend all holy energies to help me

release all which does not serve me, that I may better and more Divinely accelerate forward, serving myself as well as others.

Invitation and Permission
I invite Archangel Jophiel and the Flame Orange Ray for the Healing of Indignity, Shame, and Burning Humiliation into my heart, my soul, and all four bodies. I give my permission to fully allow Archangel Jophiel to direct the Flame Orange Light to any part of all four bodies where it is most needed. I allow the Flame Orange Light to reawaken the DNA in my physical body.

Indignity hurts. Ourselves and others. Let us consider the meaning of indignity. We suffer indignity when we feel shame, humiliation, disgrace, embarrassment, or when we feel that we somehow have dishonored ourselves or been dishonored by others.

For the healing of such experiences, and for the healing of the imprint made upon all of our selves: mental, physical, emotional and spiritual, we begin.

Find and bless your sacred space of quiet and stillness. Begin the Holy Breath. Take deep, connected breaths. Breathe Spirit and all holy energies in through the nose. Breathe distracting and/or negative energies out through the mouth.

In each breath: Spirit and peace invited in, turmoil and distraction are escorted out. Continue with this Holy Breath. *Your Friends have been standing by.*

We begin: *Archangel Jophiel, I know that whatever faith and trust I have at this moment are more than enough to invite you and the Flame Orange Ray into my heart and soul for this magnificent healing journey.*

No gentle warm orange sunsets here. Envision the *hot orange* color of flames of fire. We intend to clear, cleanse and transform all energies of shame, humiliation and indignity, and the isolating sense of unworthiness which is the consequence.

These indignities, humiliations, and shame have accumulated over a period of years—since infancy, in fact.

Archangel Jophiel and the Flame Orange Ray are, at this moment, lighting fires within you, serving two purposes:

1) The Flame Orange Ray will warm your inner being with protection and comfort for past (possibly powerful) experiences which might arise.

2) The Flame Orange Ray will toast and engulf the residual energies of those experiences, so that they go up in smoke, to be transformed by the Holy Spirit into love, as you breathe out.

If you have resistance, note and accept the resistance. Thank your ego for wanting to hold on to these past patterns and experiences, to these old energies and habits. Inform your ego: *I am moving on. I release the past and the old.*

Continue the Holy Breath. *Flame Orange Ray, seek and enfold the places in my body which are holding the experiences and consequences of shame, humiliation, indignity and frustration.*

You do not need to know where in the body these areas are, or recall or re-experience the origin of each injury. Archangel Jophiel knows where to send the Flame Orange Ray. Reminder: you are Divinely loved and protected in any moment of comfort and discomfort.

Continue to breathe. Feel the Flame Orange Ray begin in the back of your head, slowly traveling down, almost back to front.

Envision the Golden, Flame Orange glow around your head, as the Flame Orange Ray examines, seeks and illuminates each cell which is holding the experience of shame, humiliation and indignity.

The Flame Orange Ray continues its holy, liberating mission: igniting dark areas which have been hiding in shame.

These areas have believed themselves to be in a poverty of love, darkened by indignity and humiliation. Via the Flame

Orange Ray, Spirit's light heals the perception of poverty in each cell with the ever abundant wealth of unconditional love and healing. Your DNA is reawakened to its Divine value. Once the DNA is reawakened, your healing is embraced in all four bodies.

The Flame Orange Ray rests in the brain, throat, eyes, and ears—each location in your physical body, as well as your mental, emotional and spiritual bodies, where shame and indignity have been inflicted and held.

Where feelings have been hurt, where injury and insult have been absorbed and stolen the light away, the Flame Orange Ray warms and targets as a laser, encircling each cell, each molecule, with love and Orange Light, illuminating the dark, replacing the darkness with light.

The Flame Orange ray continues to heal in the heart, the mind, in all places where shame and indignity have been inflicted and suffered, sizzling and brightening.

Rest in the Flame Orange Ray, *allowing the light* to travel to each cell and do its restorative, healing work. Do not try to will or compel the healing. Simply rest and *allow*. Continue with the Holy Breath.

Indignity in the soul—let's heal it all. Indignity also occurs on a deep level in the soul. Certain thoughts and words you have expressed or received are translated into shame and rejection, wounding both your soul or perhaps another's. Let us begin the soul work.

Breathe deeply. Do not forget to breathe. You may have a sense of disquiet or you may feel unsettled in the heart area—this disquiet is the awakening of your soul wounds. These wounds have been waiting for light, and at the same time have become accustomed to the dark, in spite of their longing.

Let us now begin to replace the darkness with light. Continue to be aware of being enveloped in a field of light—the glow of the Flame Orange Ray. You are enveloped as if floating in the midst of a brightly glowing cloud. The cloud has penetrated every molecule, every DNA strand, and has penetrated to your soul.

The Flame Orange Light travels gently and lovingly through the soul, reawakening connectedness with the ONE—reigniting the connection—the spark of Spirit.

Continue to breathe. Flame Orange energies are seeking and reminding each aspect of your soul of the truth. As we complete the journey, we release the Flame Orange Ray with our gratitude.

The soul continues to heal. We thank Spirit and Archangel Jophiel for the healing and navigation of the Flame Orange Ray. We thank our selves for our willingness to be willing.

Often the rays work together in partnership. As you release the Flame Orange Ray, call forth St. Germaine and the Violet Flame of Transmutation. Continue the Holy Breath. Breathe Spirit in; breathe out any negative energies into St. Germaine's holy Violet Flame for Divine transformation.

Be conscious of the Holy Breath: *Violet Flame, transform and transmute all negative energies into the unconditional love and abundance of the Universe.*

Closing Affirmation
Whole I AM. Liberated from the old and past I AM.
Reconnected to the One I AM.
Beloved I AM. Glorious I AM. Worthy I AM.

Closing Prayer
Thank you, Archangel Jophiel, and thank you, Spirit, for transforming shame and humiliation into grace, dignity and Divine love. Thank you for my liberation from the past and the old, allowing me to move forward. Help me to continue to be aware of the abundance of love and light in each cell of my being,

in my soul, and of my One-ness. I intend to notice Your daily miracles and reminders of Your Divine Love towards myself and others, and I intend to express Divine love, dignity and compassion towards myself and others, with each breath.

Author's note: I was acutely aware of a physical process of unsettling and then resting as the Flame Orange Ray moved through me. Particularly, my heart area felt physically unsettled as the Flame Orange Ray warmed, targeted and healed. This butterfly feeling passed and was replaced by a sense of peace and rest as the Flame Orange Ray continued. The healing experience was gentle, with the presence of Archangel Jophiel keenly felt.

I was taken aback to discover the raising of angers during the healing, which needed to be blessed and released into the Violet Flame of Saint Germaine. The bless and release process into the Violet Flame was (appropriately) continuous for me.

Occasionally, I forgot the Holy Breath. Focus was recovered when I remembered to breathe, and I was able to complete the meditation.

Chapter Thirty

Platinum Ray to Cleanse, Renew and Regenerate
Holy Master, Devoted Friend Jesus, Master Illuminator

Often partnered with
Aquamarine Ray of Gentility and Grace
Used in partnership to smooth and make more gentle
the experience of other healing rays.
Lady Quan Yin, Divine Goddess of Mercy, Compassion
and Charity

Holy and Powerful. Out with the old, I
n with the new.
In order for the renewal of resurrection,
an end must first take place.
You must finish before you can begin again.

Opening Affirmation
Divinely reborn, renewed,
resurrected to a new life without limit, I AM.

Opening Prayer
Precious Jesus, I know and accept that I AM beloved by you just as I AM. I accept your Divine response to my decision, to help me break free of the old limits which hold me back, to clean

house in all four bodies, in order to begin a new, vibrant life, making room and manifesting all of the Divine gifts which you offer, in every aspect of my life. I offer you all of the trust I have as we begin this powerful and holy journey of rebirth with the Platinum Ray.

Invitation and Permission

I invite Jesus and the Platinum Ray to Cleanse, Renew, and Regenerate into my heart, my soul, and all four bodies. I give my permission to fully allow Jesus to direct the Platinum Ray to any part of all four bodies where it is most needed. I allow the Platinum Ray to reawaken the DNA in my physical body.

Jesus wants you to know: *Because I love you, unconditionally, I AM ever at your service. We have to lose, heal, release, transmute and transfigure the old, in order to make way for the new. Out with the old, in with the new.*

The purpose of the Platinum Ray is to heal, transfigure, transform, cleanse, renew, and regenerate. End habits of an old, burdened, limited way of life. Begin a new, better, fuller, richer, more present and alive life, brimming with Divine vitality in all four bodies, in every breath you breathe. It's time to clear and renew on the deepest levels.

You are ready. Perhaps you have been longing, for a long while, beloveds, for your own resurrection.

Envision brilliant White Gold. Perhaps a visit past a jeweler's window may remind you of the brilliance of Platinum energies. The Platinum Ray is the Christed Light. Seek your sacred space. Give yourself all the time you need. Begin the Holy Breath.

Jesus suggests that you take a moment and invite Lady Quan Yin first, and Her Aquamarine Ray of Gentility and Grace, to prepare for this intense healing. Jesus and Lady Quan Yin often work in Divine and delightful partnership.

Continue the Holy Breath as you follow Lady Quan Yin's meditation. Jesus, my Precious Friend, I call you forth. I call forth the Platinum Ray to Cleanse, Renew, Regenerate, to heal, transfigure, transform. He is already with you. Jesus remains with you, even after the healing is completed.

Continue to breathe. As you might stand under a warm summer rainfall, face turned up to the warmth and renewal, you are now under a concentrated laser shower of loving and intense White Gold Platinum light, streaming upon and around you.

Continue to breathe. Jesus is guiding the Platinum Ray to best serve you.

In order to make way for the new, the vital, the holy, the highest and best Divine energies in the extreme, which Jesus, Spirit and the Universe offer you, Jesus must make space, stripping away dark, crusty layers, cleansing, renewing each cell, each DNA strand, each energy which does not serve you. This Jesus does with the Platinum Ray Light.

Continue to breathe. White Gold Platinum Light, directed by Jesus, continues to flow through the body, *illuminating,* reawakening, Divinely loving, enveloping each
aspect, each cell and DNA strand, clearing, cleansing.

Continue to breathe. As each space, each cell, each DNA strand is cleared and cleaned, pierced and strained, stripped clean, Jesus renews, transfigures the old into the radiant brand new with Platinum Light.

Continue the Holy Breath. Illuminating, illuminating, the Platinum Ray and Jesus continue to move through the body. Head, throat, heart, beloveds, where so much space is taken up by energies which are not serving you. The Platinum Ray, directed by Jesus, rests, clears, cleansing, renewing, intensely and Divinely.

Continue the Holy Breath. Your entire being is shimmering, refreshed, renewed, resurrected, illuminated.

Platinum White Gold brilliance of Divine unconditional love continues to move through and transform all four bodies, illuminating mental, emotional, spiritual, physical. Breathe In Jesus and the Platinum Ray. Breathe out energies which do not serve.

Continue the Holy Breath. Jesus continues to guide the sharp edged and powerful energies of the Platinum Ray, illuminating any areas where love is not abiding. Jesus is transfiguring and (re)instilling Divine unconditional love, resurrecting, increasing your availability and receptivity to receive and express Divine gifts.

Continue the Holy Breath. Consider the meaning of regeneration—renewal, revival, rebirth. Negativity is replaced with Divine unconditional love and compassion for self and others. *As each aspect of your being is cleansed, it is immediately lovingly replenished, restored, nurtured, revived, resuscitated, reborn.*

Continue with the Holy Breath. The cleansing, the renewal, the regeneration is complete. What was dark is now light. What was exhausted is now filled with Divine vitality.

Your Friend, Master Illuminator Jesus, remains lovingly with you. The old limits have been obliterated and transformed—your resurrection is complete.

Closing Affirmation
Reborn, I AM, brimming with Divine gifts.
I AM manifesting the Divine within me in every breath.

Closing Prayer
Jesus, for my rebirth, for my reawakening to the gifts of the Divine, for my manifesting and reflecting only the deepest and highest expressions of Spirit, for your continuing and abiding

friendship, I AM grateful and I thank you. No longer trudging slowly beneath old burdens which do not serve, I AM grateful to travel reborn; lightly, swiftly, freely on the wings of Spirit.

Author's note: My experience was somewhat intense. I felt the effects of the Platinum Ray very physically—a sense of energy from behind, moving forward, and a sense of almost electric tingling which seemed to pass as the Platinum Ray mediation completed. I almost had a sense of needing to rush through the meditation, with thoughts of the day ahead. This meditation can not be rushed. I am reminded that the day ahead is in perfect order when time is offered to the Divine.

INDEX

FRIEND	HEALING RAY COLOR(S)	INTENTION and PURPOSE	PAGE
Divine White Light Totality (All the Colors of the Rays)	White Light	Clear the Path	ix
Mother Mary Queen of Angels	Pink Ray	Unconditional Love, Wisdom and Comfort	15
	Crème Soft White/Soft Yellow Rose Ray	Comfort, Empathy, Consideration, Thoughtfulness	123

Lady Quan Yin Divine Goddess of Mercy, Compassion and Charity	Aquamarine Ray	Gentility and Grace to Smooth and Make More Gentle the Healing Rays (Often used in partnership with other healing rays)	91
	Brilliant Pink Ray	Forgiveness and Absolution	21
	Amber Ray	Devotion; Healing of Disconnect and Indifference; Reestablishment of Awareness of Connection in Prayer, and Connection and Communication with Spirit in Every Moment	137
	Lavender Ray	Compassion and Nurturing	131
	Peach Ray	Invite and Experience Divine Intervention	1

Archangel Uriel Archangel of Transformation	Magenta Ray	Purity and Hope	117
	Navy Blue Ray	Healing and Elevation of Spirit	143
	Red Ray	Courage, Faith, Truth, and Hope (Divine Discernment)	155
	Indigo Ray	Success Reactivation; Release of Self-Defeating, Self-Destructive Behaviors; Knowledge of Self Worth and Indwelling Faith; Reconnection to the ONE; Activation of Faith and Belief in Oneself; Heartiness and Resilience	47
	Aqua Ray	Exaltation and Glory <u>in</u> Spirit, Exaltation and Glory <u>of</u> Spirit; We are One with Spirit	149
	Mauve Ray	Clarity of Intention	27
	Light Green Ray	Peace and Protection; Resolution of Conflict, Diminishing and Transmutation of Anger	161
St. Germaine	Violet Flame	Transmutation	9

Archangel Michael Archangel of Truth and Healing	Chartreuse Ray	Deeper into Discernment; Healing of Neglect	99
	Royal Deep Blue Ray	Peace and Prosperity	95
	Sky Blue Ray	Truth and Hope; Faith, Courage, Clarity	111
	Blue Ray	Truth, Justice, Clarity, Healing and Hope (Divine Confidence)	105
Archangel Raphael Archangel of Planetary and Personal Healing	Emerald Green Ray	Purity and Infilling of Abundance; Healing of Perception of Lack	53
	Jade Green Ray	Healing of Internal and External Injuries	59
Archangel Jophiel Archangel of Illumination	Orange Ray	Creativity	77
	Flame Orange Ray	Healing of Indignity, Shame, Burning Humiliation	175
	Yellow Ray	Reactivation of Joy	33
Archangel Zoriah Archangel of the Brilliant Rainbow	Turquoise Ray	Find an Oasis of Tranquility in the Midst of Inner and Outer Turmoil	39

Archangel Zoriel Messenger of God	Dark Pink Ray	Healing of Depression	169
	Auburn Ray	Instill and Awaken Organizational Skills and Abilities; Clearing, Cleansing, and Reorganization of Inner and Outer Clutter	83
Anarashia, Silver One As Jesus is to Gold, Anarashia is to the Silver	Silver Ray	Healing, Purity, Abundance and Joy	71
Holy Master, Devoted Friend Jesus Master Illuminator	Platinum Ray	Cleanse, Renew, Regenerate	181
Cosmic Buddha, Holy Master, Devoted Friend Jesus	Golden Ray and the Christed Light	Enlightenment Compassion, Illumination, Unconditional Love; Joyfulness and Gratitude in Every Breath	65

Author Page

Irene Lucas is a writer and editor, and has been a part of the metaphysical field for the last twenty five years. Also a video writer and producer, Irene creates and presents safety training workshops and videos to empower people with developmental disabilities. She is absolutely knocked out by the devotion, courage and dignity of her students, and by their constant successes.

When Irene presents *"30 Miracles in 30 Days"* meditation circles, workshops and speaking engagements, her greatest delight is to hear her students and audiences exclaim, *"Awesome! It works! I did it! I can't believe it is that easy!"*

After living most of her life near the sea in Santa Barbara, Irene now lives on Colorado's Front Range in Colorado Springs, and is thrilled and amazed to discover four actual seasons. She is married to her wonderful Louis, has two radiant sons, Dimitri and Alexander, and feels lucky to wake up every morning and be inspired by the Rockies.

*Irene is available for individual and group healing and coaching sessions, speaking engagements, meditation circles, and Connecting-To-The-Divine individual and group workshops. You can contact her via her website **www.theuniverseislistening.com** or email her at **irene@theuniverseislistening.com** .*

Other Books Published by
Ozark Mountain Publishing, Inc.

Conversations with Nostradamus, Volume I, II, III...............by Dolores Cannon
Jesus and the Essenes..by Dolores Cannon
They Walked with Jesus...by Dolores Cannon
Between Death and Life....................................... by Dolores Cannon
A Soul Remembers Hiroshima...by Dolores Cannon
Keepers of the Garden..by Dolores Cannon
The Legend of Starcrash...by Dolores Cannon
The Custodians...by Dolores Cannon
The Convoluted Universe - Book One, Two, Three...............by Dolores Cannon
I Have Lived Before...by Sture Lönnerstrand
The Forgotten Woman...by Arun & Sunanda Gandhi
Luck Doesn't Happen by Chance...................................by Claire Doyle Beland
Mankind - Child of the Stars.............................by Max H. Flindt & Otto Binder
The Gnostic Papers..by John V. Panella
Past Life Memories As A Confederate Soldier.........................by James H. Kent
Holiday in Heaven...by Aron Abrahamsen
Is Jehovah An E.T.?..by Dorothy Leon
The Ultimate Dictionary of Dream Language............................by Briceida Ryan
The Essenes - Children of the Light...............by Stuart Wilson & Joanna Prentis
Power of the Magdalene................................by Stuart Wilson & Joanna Prentis
Rebirth of the Oracle....................................by Justine Alessi & M. E. McMillan
Reincarnation: The View from Eternity......by O.T. Bonnett, M.D. & Greg Satre
The Divinity Factor..by Donald L. Hicks
What I Learned After Medical School ....by O.T. Bonnett, M.D.
Why Healing Happens..by O.T. Bonnett, M.D.
A Journey Into Being...by Christine Ramos, RN
Discover The Universe Within You..by Mary Letorney
Worlds Beyond Death..by Rev. Grant H. Pealer
Let's Get Natural With Herbs..by Debra Rayburn
The Enchanted Garden...by Jodi Felice
My Teachers Wear Fur Coats.........................by Susan Mack & Natalia Krawetz
Seeing True...by Ronald Chapman
Elder Gods of Antiquity...by M. Don Schorn
Legacy of the Elder Gods...by M. Don Schorn
Reincarnation...Stepping Stones of Life ....by M. Don Schorn

Continue for more books by Ozark Mountain Publishing, Inc.

Children of the Stars .... by Nikki Pattillo
Angels - The Guardians of Your Destiny ....by Maiya & Geoff Gray-Cobb
Seeds of the Soul...by Maiya Gray-Cobb
The Despiritualized Church...by Rev. Keith Bender
The Science of Knowledge ....by Vara Humphreys
The Other Side of Suicide ....by Karen Peebles
Journey Through Fear ....by Antoinette Lee Howard
Awakening To Your Creation ....by Julia Hanson

For more information about any of the above titles, soon to be released titles, or other items in our catalog, write or visit our website:

PO Box 754
Huntsville, AR 72740
www.ozarkmt.com
1-800-935-0045/479-738-2348
Wholesale Inquiries Welcome

Our Gift to You
30 Miracles in 30 Days Card Deck
&
Weekly Messages from Our Divine Friends

FREE with this certificate

Please visit our website
www.theuniverseislistening.com

Name _____
Address _____
City _____ State
_____ Zip _____ Email _____
_____

Our Gift to You
30 Miracles in 30 Days

Please visit our website
www.theuniverseislistening.com

Your own personal one hour healing session with
Holy Masters, Angels and Archangels
(by telephone)

25% off with this certificate

Name _____
Email _____

Our Gift to You
30 Miracles in 30 Days
Please visit our website **www.theuniverseislistening.com**

25% Off
Your <u>first order</u> with this certificate

SIMPLY FOR THE FUN OF IT ALL!

To correspond with each of the 30 sacred healing rays, vibrating to each unique color of light and fragrance, we have created and we offer Miracle:

Candles	Soap
Incense (cones and sticks)	Bath Oils
Essential oils	Bath Salts
Uplifting room fragrance freshener sprays	Lotion
Gift baskets & kits	

Name _____

Email _____